T0231054

Enterprise Architecture and Information Assurance

Developing a Secure Foundation

Enterprise Architecture and Information Assurance

Developing a Secure Foundation

James A. Scholz

CRC Press
Taylor & Francis Group
Boca Raton London New York

CRC Press is an imprint of the
Taylor & Francis Group, an **informa** business
AN AUERBACH BOOK

CRC Press
Taylor & Francis Group
6000 Broken Sound Parkway NW, Suite 300
Boca Raton, FL 33487-2742

© 2014 by Taylor & Francis Group, LLC
CRC Press is an imprint of Taylor & Francis Group, an Informa business

No claim to original U.S. Government works

Printed on acid-free paper
Version Date: 20130711

International Standard Book Number-13: 978-1-4398-4159-4 (Hardback)

Library of Congress Cataloging-in-Publication Data

Scholz, James A.
 Enterprise architecture and information assurance : developing a secure foundation / James A. Scholz.
       pages cm
     Includes bibliographical references and index.
     ISBN 978-1-4398-4159-4 (hardback)
     1. Database security. 2. Information storage and retrieval systems. 3. Management information systems. 4. Data protection. 5. System design. I. Title.

QA76.9.D314S34 2013
003--dc23   2013025176

Visit the Taylor & Francis Web site at
http://www.taylorandfrancis.com

and the CRC Press Web site at
http://www.crcpress.com

This book is dedicated to all those hardworking
system administrators who do not get enough recognition
for the thankless job of keeping data safe, systems
running, and development life cycles moving.
This book is dedicated to the members of the American public
who would like to understand what our government does
to secure our data and where our taxpaying dollars go in
support of the countless undisclosed amounts of data.
And of course, many thanks to my lovely wife for the hours spent
proofreading the many lines of this book to ensure that I say what
I mean, as translated from geek to lay terminology! Sue, I love you.

Contents

Preface

Within the "industry" most know, or have heard, that the requirements of the federal government and enforcement of information assurance have heightened in the past years. With the incorporation of the Gramm–Leach–Bliley Act (GLBA), the Sarbanes–Oxley Act (SOX), and the Clinger–Cohen Act, it seems that we have multiple requirements with a mixture of standards. To add to the confusion (as some may see it), we have Control Objectives for Information and related Technology (CoBit), Information Technology Infrastructure Library (ITIL), Microsoft Operations Framework (MOF), International Organization for Standardization (ISO), and other frameworks that our clients wish to incorporate into their infrastructures.

Business service management (BSM) holds many challenges; approaches to BSM, using each of the different platforms, are a little different than most organizations think and should remain that way by identifying the lowest common denominator, a piece of hardware or software, and applying that piece of equipment to the business model and its functions within the business. Asset management involves budgetary requirements under the ITIL, and it coexists with change, release, and configuration management, all of which require input into the management of an information technology (IT) system and cohesion with the configuration management database (CMDB) so the organization can get on track and meet the requirements of its governing headquarters.

The three operations required for effective IT management are as follows:

1. Portfolio management (PM)
2. Enterprise architecture (EA)
3. Capital planning and investment control (CPIC)

Each of these operations is an essential factor in relation to the total cost of ownership (TCO) and the management of investments within the infrastructure. Although some of these management functions are called something else, still they equate to an ITIL, MOF, CoBit, or ISO requirement or process. Regardless, following a secure model will save the organization millions of dollars in losses, damages, and the cost of rebuilding your data system infrastructure.

For those of you not aware of the requirements, they have all been part of the federal government and can be referenced at http://csrc.nist.gov. Pick your subject area, and you will discover expert levels of knowledge at your fingertips. The federal government has been doing this since the inception of the computer. Some who have been around for a while may remember the "Rainbow Series," "Common Criteria," and "Earned Value Management System"; these are all federal standards that date back to 1960 (I know, before some of you were born!). When in doubt about incorporation of someone's way of doing things in Enterprise Architecture (EA), Portfolio Management (PM), Capital Planning and Investment Control (CPIC), or Information Assurance (IA), reference the National Institute of Standards and Technology (NIST) and your level of understanding will be raised 100%.

Additional information is available from the CRC Press website: http://www.crcpress.com/product/isbn/9781439841594. This includes templates that will help document what you are doing and help management understand the importance of what "managing" is all about for the security of the enterprise. Security is more than just defining a few controls; these policies and procedures will assist you in becoming compliant with its many requirements, regardless of the industry. These templates are provided as an enhancement to the verbiage of the chapters and are just some of the many examples that you have full right to manipulate and adjust to meet your requirements. The templates provided cover each chapter and if you follow along with the templates after or before reading a chapter, you will receive the full benefit of your reading experience.

Each process is just a means of management, operation, or some level of technical control, and with a sound foundation of security you cannot go wrong in building your infrastructure.

Acknowledgments

Thanks go to Dr. Ron Ross, Arnold Johnson, Marianne Swanson, Peggy Hines, and the rest of the great, hardworking enthusiasts at the National Institute of Standards and Technology (NIST). NIST is a part of the Department of Commerce and under executive order defines the security standards for the federal government. These standards are free, as are many of the publications I encourage you to read and to heed the requirements as best as possible. NIST develops its documents in furtherance of its statutory responsibilities under the Federal Information Security Management Act (FISMA) of 2002, Public Law 107-347. I am a miser and do not like throwing money at a problem that can be solved with some common sense, education, and a little hard work. Don't waste your stakeholder's money; you can save thousands by educating yourself and reading some of these great manuals.

Introduction

Where or when did information security become an issue? If you look at the various ages our world has evolved through, we are now in what we call the Information Age, a period in time during which we have more data that are related to almost nothing and for which we try to account. The types of data issues we are faced with include the following:

- Classifying (not in the security sense but as in filing or archiving)
- Storing
- Setting destruction standards
- Setting sensitivity standards (personally identifiable information (PII))
- Protecting
- Moving (media bandwidth)
- Controlling—who can access it
- Needless other tasks that produce nothing

And then we have the metadata and the components that accompany it.

Reading this book will not give you just a few reasons why security is foremost, but reading it and following the procedures will give you an understanding of your infrastructure and what requires further attention.

In the Information Age we have created requirements and standards that for some are hard to understand and follow—or perhaps people are just plain lazy in doing their jobs. With the recent crash of the economy, loss of jobs, fleecing of America, and corporations' continuance to destroy America by outsourcing jobs, job security does not exist. Information assurance is and will remain the future for all the "data" created. Now you have to create a new wheel on how to meet the standards and requirements for infrastructure security. A mere review of the confidentiality, integrity, and availability is not and will never be acceptable in a world that demands privacy.

Throughout this book, I will interject my opinion about various areas and my experience in dealing with customers as a consultant and how they can manipulate you to produce more than you should or expect you to overlook what is not completed or planned for the infrastructure, or is just not happening.

Studies have shown that the enactment of the Paperwork Reduction Act (44 U.S.C. 3501 et seq.) has placed more of a burden and paper requirement on the people it was designed to protect than during any other time in history, and we produce more paper documents than ever before.

After reading this book you will have the knowledge to better understand how to evaluate your network, evaluate the business model of your company, and learn how they fit together in the selection of the correct systems to support your infrastructure. You will understand how to perform a business impact analysis and a risk assessment to further develop your data security needs. Furthermore, your knowledge of the different processes of the Information Technology Infrastructure Library (ITIL), Microsoft Operations Framework (MOF), and business service management will come to light. You will understand how they are truly derivatives of a security function that is or is not in place, and you will see how you can implement the correct level of controls for the specific process. You will also have the seed to start developing your skills to better understand the 17 families of management, how they are applied, and at what level they are applied; you will know what management, operational, and technical control is and how each are implemented within your infrastructure (Figure I.1). As a final benefit of this book, you will have the tools to

IDENTIFIER	FAMILY	CLASS
CA	Security assessment and authorization	Management
PL	Planning	Management
RA	Risk assessment	Management
SA	System and services acquisition	Management
PM	**Program management**	**Management**
AT	Awareness and training	Operational
CM	Configuration management	Operational
CP	Contingency planning	Operational
IR	Incident response	Operational
MA	Maintenance	Operational
MP	Media protection	Operational
PE	Physical and environmental protection	Operational
PS	Personnel security	Operational
SI	System and information integrity	Operational
AC	Access control	Technical
AU	Audit and accountability	Technical
IA	Identification and authentication	Technical
SC	System and communications protection	Technical

Figure I.1 Eighteen security families.

document your infrastructure to feed into the continuity of operations and disaster recovery.

Although there are 18 controls listed, the PM controls information security programs (NIST SP 800-53r3, Appendix G, "Program Management (PM) Family"). This family provides security controls at the organization rather than information system level.

Okay, you want to learn about securing the network. Hopefully you can understand the requirements as well as the process of such a tedious task.

Where do I start? I recommend you begin when the company is first decided upon and the company name has been selected. You've gone to the Secretary of State and are now registered. This is a place we all want to start from, and if you are fortunate, you were given the chance to begin your tasks here. Unfortunately, most of us start in the middle and work our way to one end or the other.

There are five basic areas to think about when designing a foundation for your security program and building your infrastructure. You really don't have to start at the beginning; it just helps the downriver processes when you know where you are. When looking at the five basic areas, you need to take into consideration each of the families of controls. As laid out previously, the controls are placed in class order and relate to the five basic areas. When you start building the foundation of your infrastructure, you need policies for everything that is done; if in doubt, write a policy. Information technology (IT) people forget about the policy and just jump right into the implementation process, building procedures as they go. This will come back to bite you when you have a compliance audit (Statement on Auditing Standards [SAS] no. 7, HIPAA, GLBA, NIST) or a restructuring phase of your infrastructure—count on it. This is especially true when dealing with database structures and software development projects. When you look at your infrastructure and what has already been accomplished, take a look at the five requirements in order and see where and how you stack up, and to what level of detail your compliance levels are. The six levels of compliance are

1. **Policy:** Applies to management buy-in and is expressed to the users.
2. **Procedure:** Pertains to the true meaning of how and why things are done this way.
3. **Implementation:** How and what plan is in place, and what documents are written.
4. **Testing:** How it works; "works fine" does not meet the criteria.
5. **Acceptance:** Does it really do what you (or they) say it should do, and does it do it efficiently and proficiently?
6. **Maintenance:** Although the maintenance phase should always be considered, I do not feel that it should be part of the compliance process, but rather a management-driven requirement to keep them involved in the security of data.

Regardless of how you lay out your project(s), have some form of logical order of events that defines each of the steps and your level of compliance with the steps. These six examples are common logical steps that take more than just the "system" into account. Enterprise architecture (EA) of all types needs to follow some template process to get from A to Z in the structure of design, management, and business services. When in doubt, improvise, adapt, and overcome!

The National Institute of Standards and Technology (NIST) is an organization within the U.S. government, under the Department of

Commerce, that has many "think tank" operators with years of experience in the enterprise architecture and security arena. The documents and processes are free and exceed those of all the other frameworks, so why develop a new wheel? I have used ITIL, Microsoft, and NIST. I always go back to NIST, not because I know it, but because it makes sense and gives you the information to design, develop, and implement a foundation that is commensurate to some of the best infrastructures in the world—you just need to stay with it and stay proactive!

Understand that the NIST "framework" is not a model but more of a practice of common sense and management by control groups and the level of responsibility for the infrastructure:

- **Management** belongs to the policy and procedures in place that dictate the way we perform functions within the architecture.
- **Operational** belongs to the way the policy and procedures are incorporated into the infrastructure and what measures are taken to ensure they work.
- **Technical** belongs to the system in which the control is implemented at the hardware or software level, a process of the hardware or the results of a software command and functions.

The certification and accreditation (C&A) process is the practical application and verification that a particular entity (government agency) has performed and met the requirements of the Federal Information Security Management Act (FISMA) by accounting for information systems, applying specific security controls, and maintaining some level of a system development life cycle (SDLC). As guides, Public Law (P.L.) 107-347 appointed NIST as a source for developing the "rules of the road" for the C&A process. Within those guidelines NIST has developed the Special Publications and Federal Information Processing Standards (FIPS) shown in Table I.1 to define and clarify the conduct of the C&A process.

Table I.1   NIST Special Publications

NIST SP 800-18	NIST SP 800-53A
NIST SP 800-30	NIST SP 800-53r3
NIST SP 800-34	NIST SP 800-60
NIST SP 800-37	NIST SP 800-128
FIPS 199/200	FIPS 140-2

There are three major factors that impact the outcome and extent of time when performing the C&A process:

1. Level of experience the provider has
2. Level of infrastructure knowledge
3. Level of cooperation provided by the client

Other factors also apply, but these three factors impart the majority of the outcomes and durations. When you look at the best practices, one must first look at the maturity level of the organization. An organization's maturity level is determined by the following five factors that are in place at the time of the evaluation:

1. Depth of policies written (what level of management buy-in is in place)
2. Level of procedures in place (determined by policy)
3. Implementation of the procedures and follow-through
4. The level of testing that has taken place to validate the procedures implemented and whether they follow policy
5. How well each of the steps is integrated into the infrastructure

Once it is determined what and how things are accomplished, a provider must look at the business model. NIST SP 800-34 defines the process of completing a business impact analysis (BIA), and this can be accomplished mentally or formally. The mental process is just a cursory review of the organization, and the provider imparts its knowledge of the organization and the NIST guidelines. For example, the Federal Bureau of Investigation (FBI) is part of the Department of Justice (DOJ), and therefore part of the executive branch of the government, which is directly governed by specific executive orders in addition to the Office of Management and Budget (OMB) and DOJ regulations and guidelines. Having background knowledge of the requirements will assist in evaluating the full business model.

Once a mental or full BIA is performed the provider can further tier the infrastructure into business units and start to draw mental boundaries of the systems. Each business unit will have certain responsibilities, and with those responsibilities the business unit is likely to have IT assets that support the unit's business model. In evaluating the business unit and adjoining IT assets, the provider should develop boundaries. NIST SP 800-37 identifies the development of boundaries and what factors need to be considered.

In the process of what has taken place so far, a provider has worked with the client and also determined the system development life cycle (SDLC) process the client is using, if any. A mature SDLC has defined security controls (SCs) for each business system and has or is in the process of applying the controls. Additionally, the client has already determined what level of confidentiality, integrity, and availability (CIA) the system must meet, and those levels are defined as high, moderate, or low. Each level is determined through a process of evaluation using FIPS 199/200 and NIST SP 800-60.

Security controls are determined first by deciding what level of CIA the systems require and second by determining what controls are applicable to the system as prescribed in NIST SP 800-53r3.

With all the data collected, the provider must now start to evaluate the level of the facility, the security controls, and the environmental controls. Once each of the areas is reviewed and defined, the provider can start to develop the system security plan (SSP), risk assessment (RA), plan of action and milestones (POA&M), and other documents as needed for compliance with FISMA.

Most providers have or are given templates to use for the evaluation process. NIST SP 800-18 has minimum requirements for the SSP, NIST SP 800-30 and 800-39 have examples and specifics for the risk assessment, and an organization will generally have a POA&M template that is used. According to the U.S. military strategy on cyberspace (formerly secret document):

> Through the process of risk management, leaders must consider risk to U.S. interests from adversaries using cyberspace to their advantage and from our own efforts to employ the global nature of cyberspace to achieve objectives in military, intelligence, and business operations.
>
> Leaders at all levels are accountable for ensuring readiness and security to the same degree as in any other domain.

Security is a process, something that you must practice, test, implement, and audit to learn and know what results are driven from its actions. Good luck and get certified—certification is a way to express your desire and motivation of becoming a better professional. Besides, you need to be a member of the club!

About the Author

James A. Scholz is a retired U.S. Army master sergeant with 35 years of experience in destroying, handling, storing, classifying, teaching, and distributing unclassified, sensitive, and classified data. His entire military career and the 17 years after have been devoted to the field of security in some form or another. After six years of running his own business, Scholz is currently a working security professional.

1

SETTING THE FOUNDATION

Setting the foundation is obtained by first documenting the security policies and procedures necessary to ensure adequate and cost-effective organizational and system security controls are implemented, across the enterprise. A sound policy delineates the security management structure and clearly assigns security responsibilities, and lays the foundation necessary to reliably measure progress and compliance. A good policy is a document that defines the security management structure and clearly assigns security responsibilities and authority by laying the foundation necessary to reliably measure progress and compliance.

To help your team understand what is planned to be accomplished, it might be a good idea to create a flowchart (if not already done) to show the link between management policy and organizational procedures, and then further map these to the technical requirements. At the same time, look at the business model and requirements, the systems that function for that business unit, and their interconnections, and draw logical boundaries around what you believe to be a functional unit system. This will be your security perimeter when you start to segment the infrastructure. Remember, the network is its own separate entity as far as boundaries go and should be a separate documentation process. By making it this way you would logically stop all your boundaries at the physical layer of your interface.

Formal procedures provide the foundation for a clear, accurate, and complete understanding of the program implementation. An understanding of the risks and related results should guide the strength of the security control and the corresponding procedures. The procedures document the implementation of and the thoroughness in which the control is applied.

Why is security the foundation of an organization? Security as the foundation builds and produces the requirements of sound management and moves the corporation toward compliance with the industry best standards and government requirements and also establishes the groundwork for other departments within an organization to follow. For each process that takes place within the corporation, security as the foundation is the main root. Let's look at some of the processes that are by-products of security as the foundation:

1. **Asset management:** By controlling the systems you gain a management process and therefore obtain accountability. This is further defined in the ability to understand your requirements and needs for software, hardware, and peripherals—this builds that property management process and makes people responsible for what they have and also gives personal ownership.

2. **Financial management:** Gained by controlling costs of your assets and projecting replacement and the breakeven point or return on investment (ROI). This also provides for a tracking mechanism that ensures that you have a cost-effective security plan and allows you to run matrixes for your investors.

3. **Risk management:** A clear product of security as measured by the threats introduced or opposing your infrastructure. Following a mature risk management framework (RMF) will assist you in developing a proactive and cost-effective architecture.

4. **Release management:** Obtained by following a systematic way of developing and documenting your software or hardware build process. This also helps if your processes are repeatable and you are seeking certification in Capability Maturity Model Integration (CMMI) or Six Sigma. Common Criteria Evaluation Assurance Levels (EALs) are great examples of setting your progression steps and compliance standards.

5. **Configuration management:** Establishes and maintains the integrity of information systems, through control of the procedures for initializing, developing, changing, and monitoring the configurations of all software and hardware products of a system. NIST SP 800-53 CM-1 through CM-9 are controls to assist you.

6. **Change management:** Having a set of specifications for a system based upon sound management that has been formally reviewed and agreed on at a point in time, and which can be changed only through change control procedures.

7. **Availability management:** Ensuring application and hardware systems are up and available for use according to the conditions of the continuity of operations, business continuity plan, or based on the recovery time/point objective (RTO/RPO). This could also be based on a service level agreement you have with a provider.

8. **Incident management:** The identification, preservation, protection, and recovery from an incident as quickly as possible. Incident management is a reactive process, but through sound procedures and practice, it can be made into an almost seamless event; diagnostics and escalation procedures are important to quickly restoring services.

9. **Capacity management:** Identifying that the business needs and services within an organization are fulfilled using a minimum of computing resources and are defined through the business model and requirements of each division, section, office, suboffice, or other entity of the organization.

10. **Personnel management:** Administrative discipline of hiring, firing, and developing employees so that they become responsible and more valuable to the organization. It includes
    a. Conducting job analyses
    b. Planning personnel needs, and recruitment
    c. Selecting the right people for the job
    d. Orienting and training
    e. Determining and managing wages and salaries
    f. Providing benefits and incentives
    g. Appraising performance
    h. Resolving disputes
    i. Communicating with all employees at all levels

Although we identify 10, you will discover as you read this book and apply the procedures that security is the true foundation, and with it you develop and grow your organization and infrastructure in a methodical process. You have a complete checks and balance of what goes on and have given the responsibility and authority to your managers. Remember, if your people don't work, fire them! Everyone should fear that he or she can be fired for poor performance, not just civilians!

2

BUILDING THE ENTERPRISE INFRASTRUCTURE

Enterprise architecture (EA) establishes the roadmap to achieve a company's mission through optimal performance of its core business processes within an efficient information technology (IT) environment and policy built on the best industry standards. Simply stated, enterprise architectures are blueprints for systematically and completely defining an organization's current (baseline) or desired (target) environment. Enterprise architectures are essential for evolving information systems and developing new systems that optimize their mission value using a proven system development life cycle and documenting the process throughout its lifetime. The process is accomplished in logical or business terms (e.g., mission, business functions, information flows, and systems environments) and technical terms (e.g., software, hardware, and communications), and includes a sequencing plan for transitioning from the baseline environment to the target environment. With this in mind, you should create a system that tracks the procurement and development process through portfolios, and each system should be identified with a specific system of record and input defined through the capital planning and investment control (CPIC) process of the portfolio management system. Furthermore, the systems should be defined segments, managers, and system categorizations to assign ownership and responsibility.

The process of defining, maintaining, and implementing these steps effectively, the institutional blueprint assists in optimizing the interdependencies and interrelationships among an organization's business operations and the underlying IT that support operations within the business units. Overall architecture experience of the government and Fortune 500 and successful moderate-sized companies has shown that without complete and enforced enterprise architecture, organizations run the risk of buying and building systems that are duplicative, incompatible, and unnecessarily costly to maintain and integrate. This was a practice of years past that crippled the progress of a lot of organizations, forcing them to downsize and almost fail due to the overabundance of the architecture and lack of management experience in portfolio and capital planning. Securing the architecture relies on the full concept of business service management, service support, and service delivery as laid out in the Information Technology Infrastructure Library (ITIL) processes, if you feel you have a need to expend the amount of funds needed to implement this model. I like the cost-effective methods of implementation of an infrastructure security and delivery model like that defined by the National Institute of Standards and Technology (NIST). In the end, your board of directors will be happier and your stakeholders will enjoy wider margins.

For EAs to be useful and provide business value, their development, implementation, and maintenance should be managed effectively. Hopefully this book will assist you in developing the required disciplines and policies to accomplish this, or at least get you to start reading and understanding that cost-effective infrastructure leads to a better bottom dollar.

One major cost-effective solution is to look at each system and place that system into a category of information and system type. The following paragraphs will assist you in determining the information and system categories.

System categorization is one of the most difficult but cost-effective tasks facing an enterprise or portfolio manager and involves the documentation of each information system and the data type of that system. It first involves a task that for the first time establishes security categories for both information types and information systems (ISs). To ease the pain and development of a system, it is a good idea to base the security categories of the IS on the potential impact on an organization, in the event something takes place that would jeopardize the information and information systems that are needed by the organization to accomplish its assigned mission, protect its assets, fulfill its legal responsibilities, maintain its day-to-day functions, and protect the data of individuals. In determining the security categories of information and information systems you must determine the overall security category (SC) using a combination of the vulnerability and threat information of both areas when assessing the risk to an organization; when determining risk look at the *probability and possibility* of a threat being exercised, and then determine your mitigation process.

To start the process let's first develop some definitions of categories for the information. The NIST has defined data in three separate areas, and I like to assess the threat and vulnerabilities associated with a fourth category, authentication, when determining the overall categories as explained:

1. **CONFIDENTIALITY**—Preserving authorized restrictions on information access and disclosure, including means for protecting personal privacy and proprietary information. (44 U.S.C., Sec. 3542)

   A loss of *confidentiality* is the unauthorized disclosure of information; information is exposed to someone that is not authorized to view it.

2. **INTEGRITY**—Guarding against improper information modification or destruction, and includes ensuring information non-repudiation and authenticity. (44 U.S.C., Sec. 3542)

   A loss of *integrity* is the unauthorized modification or destruction of information; data diddling is an example.

3. **AVAILABILITY**—Ensuring timely and reliable access to and use of information. (44 U.S.C., Sec. 3542)

   A loss of *availability* is the disruption of access to or use of information or an information system.

4. **AUTHENTICATION**—Ensuring *authorized* personnel or systems authenticate using tokens, passwords, machine code, or some other form of identification.

In recent times a complex password of 8 to 10 characters has become a thing of the past due to the ability of malicious code to infiltrate your infrastructure and steal those now weak passwords. For instance, using the password checker provided by Microsoft at https://www.microsoft.com/en-gb/security/pc-security/password-checker.aspx

shows that a password *Uqw9Bqs6!* is a medium secure password with nine characters using all the rules:

Password: ●●●●●●●●●|

Strength: Medium

1. Upper/lowercase
2. Special characters
3. Alphanumeric
4. At least eight characters

Now, adding an additional two characters to the password, making it 11 characters long, moves the strength into the strong category:

Password: ●●●●●●●●●●●|

Strength: Strong

Is it time to reteach your users to use longer passwords so they can write them down and have to look at them each time they log into the system—not recommended.

In the event you continue using a password, versus other authentication methods, teach them to use all the characters of the keyboard, and make it something they know and deal with every day. For example:

1. Using the name *Fredrick S. Smith III* and applying the rules above, take the person's name and transpose it as *Fr3dRick S. SmIth, 3rD*. Using the same Microsoft tool you get:

Password: ●●●●●●●●●●●●●●●●●●●●●●●|

Strength: BEST

2. As another example, look at using something else that your user may be familiar with. *I Drive a Plymouth Prowler* can be transposed into *1DrI^3 a Pl4M0uTh PrOw13R*.

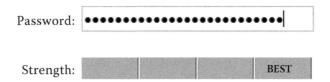

So, like everything in the information technology arena, if you train them, they can't say, "I didn't know!"

The inability to authenticate a connection leaves a system vulnerable to malicious access and loss of the information *confidentiality, integrity, and availability*.

The application of these definitions must take place within the context of each organization and the overall interest of the data being protected. NIST uses an industry standard of *low, moderate, and high* to define the overall impact; it is defined as follows:

> The potential impact is *low* if the loss of confidentiality, integrity, availability, or authentication could be expected to have a *limited* adverse effect on organizational operations, organizational assets, or individuals.
>
> The potential impact is *moderate* if the loss of confidentiality, integrity, availability, or authentication could be expected to have a *serious* adverse effect on organizational operations, organizational assets, or individuals.
>
> The potential impact is *high* if the loss of confidentiality, integrity, availability, or authentication could be expected to have a *severe or catastrophic* adverse effect on organizational operations, organizational assets, or individuals.

Security Categorization Applied to Information Types

The security category of an information type can be associated with both user information and system information and can be applicable to information in either electronic or nonelectronic form: data tapes, microfiche, or other forms of storage. It can also be used as input in considering the appropriate security category of an information system. When an organization is establishing an appropriate security category of an information type, it essentially requires determining *the potential impact* for each security objective associated with the particular information type.

The NIST generalized format for expressing the security category (SC) of an information type is:

SC information type = {(**confidentiality**, *impact*), (**integrity**, *impact*), (**availability**, *impact*), and adding the additional category of (**authentication**, *impact*)}

where the acceptable *impact* values are low, moderate, high, or not applicable. It assists in determining the overall impact the system has on the overall business model of the organization. Using the examples from NIST, a determination of the system can be defined and the system data type and system type can be associated.

> **Example**
>
> An organization manages *public information* on its web server and determines that there is no potential impact from a loss of confidentiality (i.e., confidentiality requirements are not applicable), a moderate potential impact from a loss of integrity, and a moderate potential impact from a loss of availability, with a "not applicable" to authentication, unless you have or use login data. The resulting security category of this information type is expressed as:
>
> **SC** information type = {(**confidentiality**, *NA*), (**integrity**, *moderate M*), (**availability**, *M*), and adding the additional category of (**authentication**, *NA*)}

Each of these information types poses a different level of threat to the company, and examining the business model and the information type as they apply to the business model will assist in determining the overall business risk for the exposure of that information. For example, information that is exposed on a web server needs to be validated against each data source, although NA in the model, the validation of data may pose a higher requirement of its category and also the cost of the mitigation steps to secure. With the model as explained, the system would have an overall business impact of moderate, the high-water mark for categorization. Once a system is placed into a business category, you use the model to determine what security needs are required to secure that asset. The next step is to take NIST SP 800-53 and apply the security requirements for the overall system categorization, not totally complete. Once you apply the requirements for a moderate system, you can find that some of the security controls are too much or prevent specific actions from taking place. Using the general rule does not apply in this case, and you can "roll your own" controls and assign "hybrid" or system-specific controls, as shown in the spreadsheet in the additional materials provided on the CRC website. One of the final steps in categorizing a system is to look at the system functions. To take the system categorization one more step, we can further divide the system into a general support system (GSS), a major application (MA), or a minor application (Ma). Each of these categories is determined by what it does and how it does it. Let's briefly explore the three categories:

A GSS has a "general" function within the enterprise and provides support to many assets; as a router, although a specific item, it supports the network and would be categorized as a general support network system, or the GSS network when writing to the system security plan (SSP) covered in NIST SP 800-18, along with the other documents that cover the GSS network.

A major application has a specific function within the enterprise and usually has no other reason for existence than what it does in the department it is supporting. For example, you have a specific database server that supports a department of your infrastructure and performs a specific company function, say finance, and that database does only payroll; you would categorize that system as a major application.

For a server that supports many instances of various database instances, I would categorize the system (computer and operating system) as a general support system (GSS), and each application of database instances as minor applications (Mas).

Security Categorization Applied to Information Systems

Determining the security category of an information system requires slightly more analysis and must consider the security categories of all information types resident on the information system. For an information system, the potential impact values assigned to the respective security objectives (confidentiality, integrity, availability, and authentication) shall be the highest values (i.e., high-water mark) from among those security categories that have been determined for each type of information resident on the information system.

The value of *not applicable* should not be assigned to any security objective in the context of establishing a security category for an information system. This is in recognition that there is a low minimum potential impact (i.e., low-water mark) on the loss of confidentiality, integrity, availability, and authentication for an information system due to the fundamental requirement to protect the system-level processing functions and information critical to the operation of the information system. Using Table 2.1 will assist in understanding each of the impact levels and help you decide what impact the system has on your business data and information systems.

Once you have identified your data and the system and developed your categories, you should look at what controls need to be in place to protect those data and the information system. The minimum security requirements explained in the next paragraph will identify 17 different families and control types to apply toward your data and IS. The 18th family of controls applies to the entire company and should also be considered when determining controls applied. Although not each of the controls may be required, you may have to establish a mixture of the controls to obtain your best coverage. In determining the category of a system, evaluate each of the areas of confidentiality, integrity, availability, and access (CIAA) separately and apply those controls that pertain to the data at the level you have determined to fit for the area. Each category of controls has a policy requirement, and this is supported by the five-step process of developing an enterprise using security as a model: policy; procedures; testing; implementation; and finally, monitoring or maintenance. I cannot emphasize it enough: without management buy-in, it is almost impossible to get policies to apply across the infrastructure. Take your time, be methodical, and sell security—it will pay off in the end for you, the enterprise, and the stakeholders. Using the NIST 800 series, choose the best suitable application for each of the guides and make it policy; you will provide a total cost of ownership that makes stakeholders happy. One area I cannot stress more, especially in the area of databases, is to *test* your application of controls before you apply them to the enterprise! Monitor the infrastructure and show before and after results—do the trending that supports the end value. There are many draft documents included in the additional materials provided on the CRC Press website that will assist you in the documentation process; modify them to fit your enterprise.

Table 2.1 Potential Impact

SECURITY OBJECTIVE	LOW	MODERATE	HIGH
Confidentiality			
Preserving authorized restrictions on information access and disclosure, including means for protecting personal privacy and proprietary information (44 U.S.C., Sec. 3542)	The unauthorized disclosure of information could be expected to have a *limited* adverse effect on organizational operations, organizational assets, or individuals.	The unauthorized disclosure of information could be expected to have a *serious* adverse effect on organizational operations, organizational assets, or individuals.	The unauthorized disclosure of information could be expected to have a *severe or catastrophic* adverse effect on organizational operations, organizational assets, or individuals.
Integrity			
Guarding against improper information modification or destruction, and includes ensuring information nonrepudiation and authenticity (44 U.S.C., Sec. 3542)	The unauthorized modification or destruction of information could be expected to have a *limited* adverse effect on organizational operations, organizational assets, or individuals.	The unauthorized modification or destruction of information could be expected to have a *serious* adverse effect on organizational operations, organizational assets, or individuals.	The unauthorized modification or destruction of information could be expected to have a *severe or catastrophic* adverse effect on organizational operations, organizational assets, or individuals.
Availability			
Ensuring timely and reliable access to and use of information (44 U.S.C., Sec. 3542)	The disruption of access to or use of information or an information system could be expected to have a *limited* adverse effect on organizational operations, organizational assets, or individuals.	The disruption of access to or use of information or an information system could be expected to have a *serious* adverse effect on organizational operations, organizational assets, or individuals.	The disruption of access to or use of information or an information system could be expected to have a *severe or catastrophic* adverse effect on organizational operations, organizational assets, or individuals.

(Continued)

Table 2.1 (*Continued*)   Potential Impact

SECURITY OBJECTIVE	LOW	MODERATE	HIGH
Authentication			
Ensuring that the user and systems connecting to the information for use of the data are identified	The lack of access restrictions to or use of information or an information system could be expected to have a *limited* effect on the organizational operations, organizational assets, or individuals.	The disruption of access to or use of information or an information system could be expected to have a *serious* adverse effect on organizational operations, organizational assets, or individuals.	The disruption of access to or use of information or an information system could be expected to have a *severe or catastrophic* adverse effect on organizational operations, organizational assets, or individuals.

Minimum Security Requirements

The minimum security requirements cover 17 security-related areas with regard to protecting the confidentiality, integrity, availability, and authentication of your information systems and the information processed, stored, and transmitted by those systems. The security-related areas include the following:

1. Access control
2. Awareness and training
3. Audit and accountability
4. Certification, accreditation, and security assessments
5. Configuration management
6. Contingency planning
7. Identification and authentication
8. Incident response
9. Maintenance
10. Media protection
11. Physical and environmental protection
12. Planning
13. Personnel security
14. Risk assessment
15. Systems and services acquisition
16. System and communications protection
17. System and information integrity

18. Information security programs (not included in the total count of families because it falls into the enterprise side and not the management, operational, or technical control families)

The 17 areas represent an industry-based, best-practice, balanced information security program that addresses the management, operational, and technical aspects of protecting your information and information systems. The eighteenth area covers the company and the management process to ensure that you don't get an "I didn't know" response from your users, administrators, and managers.

Policies and procedures play an important role in the effective implementation of enterprise-wide information security programs within the organization and the success of the resulting security measures employed to protect the information and information systems. Thus, organizations must develop and promulgate formal, documented policies and procedures governing the minimum security requirements and must ensure their effective implementation, through testing, in order to develop and sustain an industry standard information security program. Using the five-step process helps you ensure you follow sound practice:

1. Policy
2. Procedures
3. Testing
4. Implementation
5. Maintenance or management

Specifications for Minimum Security Requirements

The definitions, for the most part, are excerpts from NIST SP 800-53 r3 and are best-practice requirements. Although the guides are recommended, it should be mandatory at all levels of every enterprise to ensure that we protect people, assets, and business data.

Access control (AC): Organizations must limit information system access to authorized users, processes acting on behalf of authorized users, or devices (including other information systems) and to the types of transactions and functions that authorized users are permitted to exercise. Access control can be further implanted at the machine level, and access control procedures implemented for what systems are allowed as an inter/intraconnection.

Awareness and training (AT): Organizations must
1. Ensure that managers and users of organizational information systems are made aware of the security risks associated with their activities and of the applicable laws, directives, policies, standards, instructions, regulations, or procedures related to the security of organizational information systems.
2. Ensure that organizational personnel are adequately trained to carry out their assigned information security-related duties and responsibilities.

Audit and accountability (AU): Organizations must
1. Create, protect, and retain information system audit records to the extent needed to enable the monitoring, analysis, investigation, and reporting of unlawful, unauthorized, or inappropriate information system activity.
2. Ensure that the actions of individual information system users can be uniquely traced to those users so they can be held accountable for their actions.
3. Provide an automated method of performing trend analysis and report trends to portfolio managers at least quarterly.

Compliance and security assessments (CA): Organizations must
1. Periodically assess the security controls in organizational information systems to determine if the controls are effective in their application.
2. Develop and implement plans of action designed to correct deficiencies and reduce or eliminate vulnerabilities in organizational information systems.
3. Authorize the operation of organizational information systems and any associated information system connections.
4. Monitor information system security controls on an ongoing basis to ensure the continued effectiveness of the controls.

Configuration management (CM): Organizations must

1. Establish and maintain baseline configurations and inventories of organizational information systems (including hardware, software, firmware, and documentation) throughout the respective system development life cycles.
2. Establish and enforce security configuration settings for information technology products employed in organizational information systems.

Contingency planning (CP): Organizations must establish, maintain, and effectively implement plans for emergency response, backup operations, and postdisaster recovery for organizational information systems to ensure the availability of critical information resources and continuity of operations in emergency situations.

A lot of companies are moving away from tape backups; tapes are extremely costly and unreliable. Current technology trends are driving companies to the cloud; the cloud provides for another option, but possibly not the most cost-effective in security or overall costs. Virtual tape systems are getting better, and with the use of dense wave data multiplexing (DWDM) and lighting dark fiber, give an organization many more familiar options using Tivoli Storage Manager (TSM).

Identification and authentication (IA): Organizations must identify information system users, processes acting on behalf of users, or devices and authenticate (or verify) the identities of those users, processes, or devices, as a prerequisite to allowing access to organizational information systems. Remote offices (extranets, metropolitan infrastructures) and other remote architectures should use end-to-end encryption on their connections and set up local domain controllers/servers to cut down on bandwidth use and afford another level of security.

Incident response (IR): Organizations must

1. Establish an operational incident handling capability for organizational information systems that includes adequate

preparation, detection, analysis, containment, recovery, and user response activities.
2. Track, document, and report incidents to appropriate organizational officials or authorities.
3. Develop a proactive approach to network monitoring by using active tools that allow an administrator to kill traffic in its tracks.

Maintenance (MA): Organizations must
1. Perform periodic and timely maintenance on organizational information systems.
2. Provide effective controls on the tools, techniques, mechanisms, and personnel used to conduct information system maintenance.
3. Develop definitive support agreements with providers that clearly lay out the provider's responsibility in performing maintenance; ensure that cleared, reliable, trustworthy contractors are performing the work.

Media protection (MP): Organizations must
1. Protect information system media, both paper and digital.
2. Create document-marking procedures and divisional logical unit numbers (LUNs) for the data types within the storage array.
3. Limit access to information on information system media to authorized users.
4. Sanitize or destroy information system media before disposal or release for reuse, and never reuse old storage media that was previously classified in an unclassified environment.

Physical and environmental protection (PE): Organizations must
1. Limit physical access to information systems, equipment, and the respective operating environments to authorized individuals.
2. Protect the physical plant and support infrastructure for information systems.
3. Provide supporting utilities for information systems that ensure redundancy.

4. Protect information systems against environmental hazards.
5. Provide appropriate environmental controls (HVAC, fire, smoke, and security) in facilities containing information systems.

Planning (PL): Organizations must develop, document, periodically update, and implement security plans for organizational information systems that describe the security controls in place or planned for the information systems and the rules of behavior for individuals accessing the information systems.

Personnel security (PS): Organizations must
1. Ensure that individuals occupying positions of responsibility within organizations (including third-party service providers) are trustworthy and meet established security criteria for those positions.
2. Develop a risk matrix for employees' position categorization and balance against the enterprise risk acceptance levels.
3. Ensure that organizational information and information systems are protected during and after personnel actions such as terminations and transfers.
4. Employ formal sanctions for personnel failing to comply with organizational security policies and procedures.

Risk assessment (RA): Organizations must assess the risk to organizational operations (including mission, functions, image, or reputation), organizational assets, and individuals, resulting from the operation of organizational information systems and the associated processing, storage, or transmission of organizational information. The assessment process must establish a baseline of threats and vulnerabilities and the threats be assessed annually to establish your protection levels for personnel, assets, and security procedures.

System and services acquisition (SA): Organizations must
1. Allocate sufficient resources to adequately protect organizational information systems.
2. Employ system development life cycle processes that incorporate information security considerations.

3. Employ software usage and installation.
4. Ensure that third-party providers employ adequate security measures to protect information, applications, or services outsourced from the organization.

System and communications protection (SC): Organizations must

1. Monitor, control, and protect organizational communications (i.e., information transmitted or received by organizational information systems) at the external boundaries and key internal boundaries of the information systems.
2. Employ architectural designs, software development techniques, and systems engineering principles that promote effective information security within organizational information systems.

System and information integrity (SI): Organizations must

1. Identify, report, and correct information and information system flaws in a timely manner.
2. Provide protection from malicious code at appropriate locations within organizational information systems.
3. Monitor information system security alerts and advisories and take appropriate actions in response.

Security Control Selection

Leaders must consider risk. It is through the thorough process of understanding threat that you develop your strategies and mitigation process. Adapting a disposition of "we are secure, the IT department handles all that" is a herd of sheep surrounded by wolves attitude. Risk is prevalent throughout the entire organization, and leaders must learn to plan, establish the standards, and develop procedures within the organization with follow-up. This is the application of due diligence and due care.

- Due care: The steps within the procedures that are taken to identify that the organization has taken a level of responsibility for the actions that take place within the company and has applied the proper security controls necessary to help protect the company, its resources, and employees.

- Due diligence: Monitoring activities that take place to ensure the security controls are continually maintained and operational.

Through the process of risk management, leaders must consider the level of risk to the corporate interests, your adversaries, 70% of which still remain internal and are using cyberspace to their advantage to overcome the misconfigurations and weakest links to overcome your greatest efforts to obtain access to your secrets.

Through your best efforts of operational plans development, reviewing the combination of threats, vulnerabilities, and impacts, you begin to develop and identify the important trends of your infrastructure and decide where best efforts should be applied to eliminate or reduce threat capabilities; eliminate or reduce vulnerabilities; and evaluate, coordinate, and reduce all cyberspace operations.

3
INFRASTRUCTURE SECURITY MODEL COMPONENTS

In his 2012 article, titled "FBI: High-Tech Economic Espionage a Vast, Expanding Threat," Michael Cooney raised concerns about the U.S. economy and the ease of cyber theft.[*] Companies today work in a much more dynamic international trade market, in which securing that infrastructure and infrastructure components is much more complicated. Cyber-attacks have risen to unparalleled extremes. The impending threat and the way we create secure environments will change, or businesses will go under as a result of fines, malicious activity, and untethered loose ends. Successful security architecture follows a repeatable process of the following:

1. **Policy:** Management *must* buy in or you will never get the projects off the ground.
2. **Procedures:** Must be in place in the form of desktop procedures (living documents) that are updated frequently.
3. **Testing:** Before implementing something it must be tested— changes, software, updates, or new systems.
4. **Implementation:** Follow sound industry standards; don't recreate the wheel.
5. **Continuous monitoring:** How do you know what is going on and what needs to happen? If you don't, a new system on the network may be too much for the current bandwidth!

Each of these combines management, operational, and technological aspects of the infrastructure based on security as the foundation. As an information technology (IT) professional it is management's responsibility to ensure your users have a sound education and awareness

---

[*] Cooney, M. 2012. FBI: High-Tech Economic Espionage a Vast, Expanding Threat. *NetworkWorld*. Accessed from http://www.networkworld.com/community/blog/fbi-high-tech-economic-espionage-vast-expanding-threat?page=0%2C1.

program available to them, and that it is updated at least annually and documented within the corporate training files. The key foundation for implementation of these components together to meet the standards set forth in the policies is the security architecture. No other architecture model builds on security as the foundation, and as you will see in this book, everything is a by-product of security.

Each industry wants to believe that it is different from the others; its needs may be different, but the process of security and construction of the network follows the same procedures and equipment requirements. The security architecture must provide a framework for integrating existing protocols, products, and tools to meet its needs, as well as accommodate new and existing information technology systems and migration paths and anticipate future business directions. Every architecture should have a near-term, and future plan on the infrastructure and its progression. Although it may be difficult to identify actual hardware, the corporate growth should be viewed and a gap analysis performed to determine where you are, where you want to be, and how you are reaching that point.

Security should be the foundation for the entire process, and you must also consider the earned value management and portfolio management process in developing that gap. Every division, department, section, and office has specific requirements for information technology (IT) processing. As part of that gap, it needs to be identified and documented. *Although many areas of a corporation may need financial data, they do not need their own financial system; write once and read many should be followed to any extent possible.* Create groups and assign personnel to the groups, and then assign permissions to assets. A logical and documented process should be developed for each type of systems in use so system administrators can follow the repeatable process every time!

Developing the Security Architecture Model

Using security as your enterprise architecture model affords a flexible, changeable, and securable solution. What is required of an organization to develop the security architecture model tailored to your organization? Here are some basic points of interest to start your security architecture model:

1. Means of communication, Internet Protocol (IP)
2. Your communications transport mechanism, cable

3. Network infrastructure (routers, switches, firewalls, intrusion protection/detection)
4. Computer hardware
5. Computer software
6. Trusted and untrusted zones (DMZs, segments, extranets, intranets, and Internet connections)
7. Border and core access points (VPN concentrators, routers, identity access management, etc.)

Starting with the basics of architecture, Figure 3.1 identifies the five basic components of Internet Protocol security and the flow of traffic using the seven-layer Open System Interface (OSI) model. The following five bullets represent the flow of secure traffic over the OSI model:

- **Authentication:** The property of knowing that the data received are the same as the data that were sent and that the claimed sender is in fact the actual sender
- **Integrity:** The property of ensuring that data are transmitted from source to destination without undetected alteration; what you receive is what was transmitted
- **Confidentiality:** The property of communicating such that the intended recipients know what was being sent, but unintended parties cannot determine what was sent
- **Encryption:** The mechanism commonly used to provide confidentiality
- **Availability:** The rate at which a system's uptime can be reliably available to process data

In determining traffic flow the network manager must perform traffic analysis of network traffic flow for the purpose of determining the flow of information that is useful to an adversary. Examples of such information are frequency of transmission, the identities of the conversing parties, sizes of packets, flow identifiers used, etc. Request for Comments (RFC) 1825 identifies key points to consider when providing the level of security needed for your IPv4 and IPv6 traffic. RFC 1825 goes on to explain:

These headers are the "IP Authentication Header (AH)" and the "IP Encapsulating Security Payload (ESP)" header. There are a number

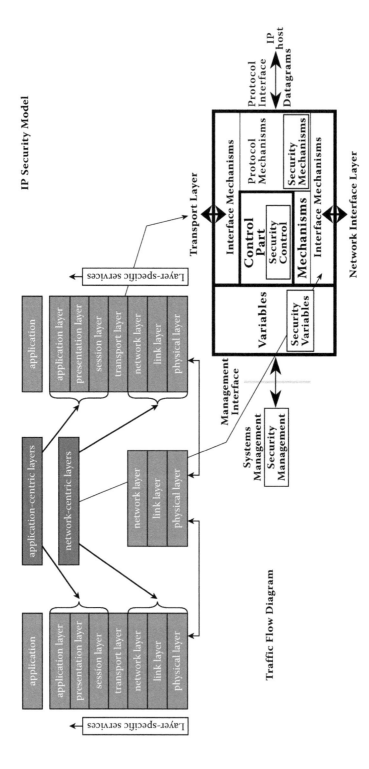

Figure 3.1 Traffic flow diagram.

of ways in which these IP security mechanisms might be used. This section describes some of the more likely uses. These descriptions are not complete or exhaustive. Other uses can also be envisioned.

The IP Authentication Header is designed to provide integrity and authentication without confidentiality to IP datagrams. The lack of confidentiality ensures that implementations of the Authentication Header will be widely available on the Internet, even in locations where the export, import, or use of encryption to provide confidentiality is regulated. The Authentication Header supports security between two or more hosts implementing AH, between two or more gateways implementing AH, and between a host or gateways implementing AH and a set of hosts or gateways. A security gateway is a system which acts as the communications gateway between external untrusted systems and trusted hosts on their own sub-network. It also provides security services for the trusted hosts when they communicate with the external untrusted systems. A trusted sub-network contains hosts and routers that trust each other not to engage in active or passive attacks and trust that the underlying communications channel (e.g., an Ethernet) isn't being attacked.

In the case where a security gateway is providing services on behalf of one or more hosts on a trusted subnet, the security gateway is responsible for establishing the security association on behalf of its trusted host and for providing security services between the security gateway and the external system(s). In this case, only the gateway need implement AH, while all of the systems behind the gateway on the trusted subnet may take advantage of AH services between the gateway and external systems.

A security gateway which receives a datagram containing a recognized sensitivity label, for example IPSO, from a trusted host should take that label's value into consideration when creating/selecting a Security Association for use with AH between the gateway and the external destination. In such an environment, a gateway which receives an IP packet containing the IP Encapsulating Security Payload (ESP) should add appropriate authentication, including implicit (i.e., contained in the Security Association used) or explicit label information (e.g., IPSO), for the decrypted packet that it forwards to the trusted host that is the ultimate destination. The IP Authentication Header should always be used on packets containing explicit sensitivity labels to ensure end-to-end label integrity. In environments using security gateways, those gateways MUST perform address-based IP packet filtering on unauthenticated packets purporting to be from a system known to be using IP security.

The IP Encapsulating Security Payload (ESP) is designed to provide integrity, authentication, and confidentiality to IP datagrams.

Dataflow Defense

Information security and building your enterprise foundation start with the basics. Here is a basic list of the defense-in-depth dataflow:

1. Protocol (IP)
2. Protocol interface (hardware)
3. Protocol interface (application)
4. Protocol transport mechanism (cable, fiber, wireless)
5. Protocol encryption
6. Transport mechanisms:
    a. Access switches
    b. Distribution switches
    c. Core switches

When considering your architecture design you must consider all the hardware and all the software that interact with your transport mechanisms. Starting with the core of your enterprise gives you the flexibility to develop technical policy and procedures as your traffic progresses through and out your infrastructure. You need to look at all the options and apply what works for your business model and business systems. Current technologies allow firewall placements at all levels of the OSI model.

The platform (mainframe, mid-systems, or Intel-based) will obviously determine how you can apply your security. In a mainframe situation you may decide to incorporate encryption at the hardware level, and that would take a hardware security module (HSM) and possibly a software engineer to write the encryption code, or you can obtain it from a vendor. The Intel platform may require a processor that has enabled encryption, two-factor authentication, and PC isolation for systems that become infected. The level of protection you provide should be scaled to the data you are trying to protect. Look at the business model and make your determination from it and the input of technical managers.

The National Institute of Standards and Technology (NIST) provides an entire series on selecting and developing your infrastructure using security as the foundation; you just need to incorporate what you need where you need it most. The application of due care and due diligence is the corporation's responsibility. To examine the NIST documents, visit http://csrc.nist.gov/publications/PubsSPs.html.

An in-depth knowledge of the systems, their interconnections, and their business function will be a vital component of the layered security architecture. Identifying the dataflow requires the identification and classification of workflow-related interconnections, and will assist in defining information system interconnections and developing your business model boundaries. To couple with this, you need to look at the next step: data in transit, date in motion, and data at rest, all of which are based upon the business impact analysis and the business function of each system.

Data in Transit, Data in Motion, and Data at Rest

The application of due diligence and due care includes the regulation, management, and protection of sensitive data against disclosure, theft, and malicious intent. That is why in further protection layers we assign permissions for access to specific data that afford a level of protection to all data types, regardless of their destination.

With the extent of laws, regulations, and industry-specific requirements from the government and public sector, compliance can provide little return on investment (ROI) for organizations and is a direct requirement of the industry regulatory setting. Although each specific regulatory requirement identifies the need or mandate, they all share common objectives toward ensuring the integrity, confidentiality, availability, and access of data, as well as the verified security of the supporting interconnecting systems and enterprise resources. In the future, within the United States all government entities will follow one guideline, that established by NIST. Figure 3.2 shows what NIST, with contributions from the industry, has developed for building your infrastructure using security as the model.

Although some say it is an expensive endeavor to provide the required level of protection mandated, look at what your company is worth, your client's data are worth, and the personally identifiable

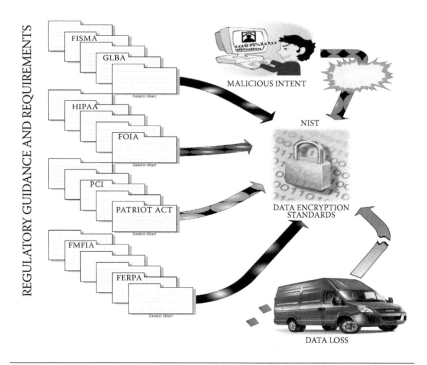

Figure 3.2   Building infrastructure using security as the model.

information (PII) is worth. Consider the lawsuits, humiliation, and global loss of business, if not your career!

Through layered application of data encryption the organization affords the data the level of protection essential to the application of due diligence and due care. The requirements cannot be ignored, as the consequences of ignorance and disregarding the need can have sweeping effects on not only a company's finances but also its reputation. Read the daily security newsletters; you continue to see headlines such as "Cyber Chief Warns of Rising Danger from Cyber Attacks." We are just now seeing the beginning of what the information age has seen in malicious activity and growing cyber espionage. Compliance and breach disclosures place a great deal of responsibility in the laps of executive management and IT professionals. Organizations have a responsibility to consider all of the potential damage that can be done to their business if sensitive data are compromised. Forget the loss of sales and customer confidence, negative publicity, and stock devaluation; these will drive your organization into bankruptcy. You must consider the damage invoked on the individuals and the civil and criminal penalties that will be imposed and wagered against you and your organization.

NIST offers five things to consider when applying encryption:

1. Consider solutions that use existing features and infrastructure of your information technology systems. Some encryption solutions require that you deploy servers and install client software on the devices to be protected, while others can use existing servers and software already present on the devices. Some operating systems include encryption features approved under the Federal Information Processing Standard (FIPS). Generally, the more extensive the changes required to the infrastructure and devices, the more likely it is that the solution will interfere with functionality or create other problems with the devices. Compare loss of functionality with gains in security and decide if the trade-off is acceptable.

2. Use centralized management for all deployments of storage encryption except for stand-alone and very small-scale deployments. Centralized management is recommended for storage encryption because it enables efficient policy verification and enforcement, key management, authenticator management, data recovery, and other management tasks. It also can automate deployment and configuration of encryption software, distribution and installation of updates, collection and review of logs, and recovery of information from local failures.

3. Ensure that cryptographic keys are secured and managed properly. Encryption technologies use one or more cryptographic keys to encrypt and decrypt data. If a key is lost or damaged, data stored on the computer could be lost, so you need to thoroughly plan key processes, procedures, and technologies. This should include all aspects of key management, including key generation, use, storage, recovery and destruction. Consider how to support the recovery of encrypted data if a key is destroyed or becomes unavailable. Also consider how changing keys will affect access to encrypted data on removable media and develop feasible solutions, such as retaining the previous keys in case they are needed.

4. Select appropriate user authenticators. Common authentication mechanisms include passwords or personal identification

numbers, cryptographic tokens, biometrics and smart cards. Consider using existing enterprise authentication tools such as Active Directory or a public-key infrastructure instead of adding another authenticator for users. This usually is acceptable if two-factor authentication already is being used. Organizations should not use any passwords that are transmitted in plain text as single-factor authenticators for encryption.

5. Take steps that support and complement encryption implementations. Storage encryption by itself cannot provide adequate security. Select additional controls based on the categories for the potential impact of a security breach on a particular system outlined in FIPS 199 and NIST SP 800-53's recommendations for minimum security controls. Supporting controls include

   - Revising organizational policies to incorporate use of the storage encryption.
   - Properly securing and maintaining user devices to reduce the risk of compromise, including securing operating systems, applications and communications, as well as physically securing devices.
   - Making users aware of responsibilities for encrypting sensitive files, physically protecting devices and removable media, and promptly reporting loss or theft.

Building a secure infrastructure is more difficult than it used to be; whereas previously we could set up a router with an access list or stick a firewall behind our core router, now building a secure infrastructure requires an in-depth view, some trial and error, and a whole lot more.

Next we will look at the network portions of the infrastructure and continue to progress through the security model of infrastructure security.

Network

Network security architecture is the next logical step in the planning and design of the network to reduce security risks. First, you need to know what threat agent you are trying to protect from, and one way to obtain these data is to perform a risk analysis and review the organization security policies. Chapter 6 goes more into the performance of a risk assessment and focuses on reducing security risks and enforcing policy. The outcome of your assessment will be to design and configure the network appliances and software security products to mitigate the threat agents or accept the level of risk imposed. When reviewing your infrastructure, you need to keep in mind that your office is heterogeneous, as applicable, and this may require you to include

- Extranets
- Telecommuting clients
- The cloud
- Other networks for which you have trusted paths established

Network security is the transport mechanism of your core transport protocols and is the main channel in which to enforce the policies and procedures developed by the managers to protect information. The network, often referred to as the "front door" in broader discussions of IT security, should be restrictive, cost-effective, and well designed. The extent of effort that you place in the design affords you the ability to reduce a threat from having the ability to introduce a malicious agent, in that it gives you the ability to block network access at the device or a computer and provide better protection for users and the enterprise.

Old-style network design focused on creating a secure network perimeter around the organization by strategically placing a firewall at the point where the network is connected to the Internet and possibly a few points within the organization.

In an extranet view, the traditional design is challenging; as a remote entity of the organization, it needs access to a large number of systems and services within the organization. Additionally, as an extranet office and because of the frequent use of contract employees, computers within the remote office cannot implicitly be trusted. This places an additional concern about security threats from inside the perimeter that are protected by the infrastructure. These design issues require a different approach to network security. Although it is impossible to do justice to the topic of network design in this chapter, some best practices are identified that focus on network design:

- Step 1: Reduce or eliminate legacy equipment that are unmanaged and configurable; legacy network devices can be used as a collection point and can be used by the "internal" threat. Removal of these devices and replacing them with managed devices limits traffic flow and further allows for port-level security at the access level.

- Step 2: Embrace the concept of defense in depth; this gives you the ability to install secondary firewalls or more restrictive access controls at the access level.
- Step 3: Take advantage of intrusion detection and intrusion prevention systems (IDSs/IPSs).
  - An intrusion detection system (IDS) looks at the incoming network traffic for signature-based patterns that can signify that a person is probing your network for vulnerable computers. The IDS can also look at traffic leaving your network for patterns that might indicate that a computer's security has been compromised. This should be an edge device and is usually the first step in attempting to compromise the security of a computer on your network.
  - Intrusion prevention systems are placed in line and are able to actively prevent/block intrusions that are detected. IPSs are also known as intrusion detection and prevention systems (IDPSs). These are network security appliances that monitor network or system activities for malicious activity; they can also be signature based in a hardware or software configuration. The main functions of intrusion prevention systems are to identify malicious activity, log information about said activity, attempt to block/stop activity, and report activity.
- Step 4: Take advantage of hardware and software virtual private networks (VPNs). This is a point-to-point encrypted channel that can be used for most external connections, but depending on your budget, it may be restrictive. A remote access server (RAS) can also be used in conjunction with the Point-to-Point Tunneling Protocol (PPTP) to allow for a limited-use remote access point from the DMZ into limited resources like email, Instant Messenger (IM), and other communication channels.
- Step 5: Network traffic statistics: Do I need to say more? Collecting the statistics of your network traffic is not only a good thing, but it gives you justification for more bandwidth,

different equipment (for bottlenecks), and more devices, if needed, to secure a specific area of issue. Monitoring and analyzing the traffic will identify a network interface that might have gone rogue, someone that is downloading large files (music/videos), or a computer that was compromised.

No one can ever guarantee security; collectively the steps provide a good starting point for improving an organization's network security.

Client-Side Security

Client-side systems should be placed at the access level of the organization using an access-level switch. Once the switch is placed for each of the various divisions, it makes it easier to create virtual local area networks (VLANs) to direct that traffic where it needs to go, and also gives you the ability to segment the division further to allow access to other segments (VLANs) by media access control (MAC) or through the Internet Protocol (IP). Most current technologies allow you to "micromanage" each segment; this is also a good point to place an IDS/IPS client, yes, monitor and control internal traffic. For years the FBI has documented that 70% of all malicious activity on a network is from internal users.

A client or host computer is often the target of internal and external threats and poses the biggest security issue to your infrastructure. Once a client has been compromised, a number of things can take place:

1. The computer can be used as a file storage site for malicious groups sharing malicious tools and other material.
2. Sensitive information stored on the computer (such as social security numbers or credit card information) can be accessed and released.
3. The host may be used as an intermediary to probe other machines for security flaws.
4. The machine may be used to launch an outright attack on other systems.

Client or host-based security can be accomplished through a well-planned template for building systems and good system administration practices, such as

- Organizing users by duty position and sections they work in
- Assigning users to groups and then assigning permissions
- Assigning network shares for document folders and limiting access permissions
- Maintaining up-to-date virus protection
- Making certain that the operating system software is configured properly
- Ensuring that all of the latest security patches are installed

The challenge is that most organizations have many clients/hosts, and without proper guidelines and procedures, management of these systems can become a nightmare. Here are some industry standards that should promote enhanced client/host-based security:

Step 1: Perform a risk assessment to identify computers by mission levels of importance. In designing a client/host-based security plan, the first step is to perform a risk assessment (Chapter 6) to determine which hosts are the most important to protect and to focus first on those computers. In general, this will include computers that provide critical IT functions such as administrative systems, financial management, human relations, and other key aspects of the organization. Create a backup option for DR and data protection for specific data, and train users on how and what goes into the backup drive space.

Step 2: Build a domain-level install template that applies to the biggest number of systems on the domain.

Step 3: Build a template for nondomain clients or stand-alone clients/hosts. *Note*: For all the client/host computers, within your build templates you should consider the following:
  - Disabling network services that are not needed.
  - Disabling all installed software services.
  - Disabling all "unnecessary services." What are unnecessary services? Here is a list of services that may be set to manual in Windows 7:
    - Application Experience
    - Computer Browser
    - Desktop Window Manager Session Manager
    - Diagnostic Policy Service

- – Distributed Link Tracking Client
- – IP Helper
- – Offline Files
- – Portable Device Enumerator Service
- – Print Spooler
- – Protected Storage
- – Remote Registry
- – Secondary Logon
- – Security Center
- – Server
- – Tablet PC Input Service
- – TCP/IP NetBIOS Helper
- – Themes
- – Windows Error Reporting Service
- – Windows Media Center Service Launcher
- – Windows Search
- • Windows Time

Note: Microsoft, as well as Defense Information Systems Agency (DISA), provides specific guidance for configuration of a secure workstation. Consider using the Security Configuration Editor (SCE) for automating your initial configuration template. The SCE gives you .inf files that are easily configurable to "roll your own" security configuration along with the DISA guidelines.

Consider running a host-based firewall, standard in Windows XP and Windows 7.

Step 4: Maintain a proper inventory of all software and hardware items.

Step 5: Establish an antivirus (AV) protection policy and procedures manual with an automated update server and build that into a separate VLAN pointing all systems to it for updates. Establish a policy for the AV server to fetch updates for .dat files at least four times each day, and a client/host policy to update at peak periods, 10 a.m., 12 p.m., 2 p.m., and 10 p.m.; each of these times are generally break times, lunch, and after-work hours. Malware, viruses, and worms were the most common security problem. Although viruses can be written for any operating system, most are written to reach the widest audience and exploit security flaws in Microsoft and Microsoft-based products.

Enterprise products afford automated updates and central management and are a requirement for virus protection software. This allows the organization to automatically update all computers running the virus protection software at specific times throughout the day and also gives you the capability to build an antivirus VLAN that segments your bandwidth and allows an efficient means of monitoring activity.

Although this option is more expensive, without this automatic update a virus may attack and do considerable damage before people have updated their virus protection software. Today's system infections spread through the Internet, email, and web, and can quickly spread and infect your entire network before you know it happened. Furthermore, creating VLANs or specific network segments isolates the outbreak to prevent organization-wide outbreaks.

Additional policies that define external media scanning on stand-alone media systems, preventing downloads of untrusted sources, and many other user restrictions that do not interfere with the daily operations are sound practices.

Step 6: Use a network scanner to create a profile for client computers you have identified. The profile should be specific for the operating system and the different services and software accessible through the network. Almost every vendor has the ability to produce a "trusted facility manual" that identifies how and what port the software uses, plus each network service on a machine is associated with a specific Transmission Control Protocol/Internet Protocol (TCP/IP) port number. Within smaller organizations it may be possible to examine the machines individually and get this information, but most organizations will want to use an automated tool to detect this information.

Step 7: Monitor security alerts and develop a solid automated process for patching systems. Most operating systems have an automated feature, regardless; the new patches should be tested quickly and then applied. In larger infrastructures with established configuration control boards/change management boards (CCBs/CMBs) or even a technical review board (TRB), this process can take up to and sometimes beyond 30 days. In most cases the risk will need to be weighed over the threat. Security alert services are available to track security problems for a fee and save a lot of research time. It is critical that a person, section within the IT infrastructure, or team be assigned to monitor these security alerts. Once a security alert is announced, you can identify what critical systems or enclaves are vulnerable and work to get the security patch installed on those systems. If the systems you are tracking number in the hundreds or beyond, you should look at tools that can help automate the process of updating the machines. Many free as well as commercial tools are available that can assist with this task. The important thing is to make certain your staff has a plan for updating these machines rapidly when a security alert is announced. A rapid response to a security alert is to reset the VLAN or border router/firewall to block access to certain network services to elude your client/host systems becoming vulnerable to a new threat. Although this may have an impact on usage, it may not be preferable for the systems to have their security compromised and to have to deal with the entire mitigation process. Personnel time and efforts need to have a value placed on the cost of automating the mitigation process!

Step 8: Create a centralized system logging service. Organizations should establish policies and procedures for log management. To establish and maintain successful log management activities, an organization should develop standard processes for performing log management. As part of the planning process, an organization should define its logging requirements and goals. Based on those, an organization should then develop policies that clearly define mandatory requirements and suggested recommendations for log management activities, including log generation, transmission, storage, analysis, and disposal. An organization should also ensure that related policies and procedures incorporate and support the log management requirements and recommendations. The organization's management must provide the necessary support for the efforts involving log management planning, policy, and procedures development.

Requirements and recommendations for logging should be created in conjunction with a detailed analysis of the technology and resources needed to implement and maintain them, their security implications and value, and the regulations and laws to which the organization is subject (e.g., FISMA, HIPAA, SOX). Generally, organizations should require logging and analyzing the data that are of greatest importance, and also have nonmandatory recommendations for which other types and sources of data should be logged and analyzed if time and resources permit. In some cases, organizations choose to have all or nearly all log data generated and stored for at least a short period of time in case it is needed, which favors security considerations over usability and resource usage, and also allows for better decision making in some cases. When establishing requirements and recommendations, organizations should strive to be flexible since each system is different and will log different amounts of data than other systems.

The organization's policies and procedures should also address the preservation of original logs. Many organizations send copies of network traffic logs to centralized devices, as well as use tools that analyze and interpret network traffic. In cases where logs may be needed as evidence, organizations may wish to acquire copies of the original log files, centralized log files, and interpreted log data, in the event there are any questions regarding the reliability of the copying and interpretation processes. Retaining logs for evidence may involve the use of different forms of storage and different processes, such as additional restrictions on access to the records.

Most major operating systems provide support for remote system logging. These system logs record each time a network service is accessed and the success or failure of that access. Usually the record contains a time stamp, event identity information, and the network service accessed. By default, these system logs are written to the local disk on the computer providing that network service; these should be configured to write their logs to a central server via the network. Once established, the logs should be limited to access and a limited number of administrators assigned to perform the trends analysis, event tracking and evaluation, and a number of other reports that can be associated with good log management.

Organizations also may store and analyze certain logs to comply with federal legislation and regulations, including the Federal Information Security Management Act of 2002 (FISMA), the Health Insurance Portability and Accountability Act of 1996 (HIPAA), the Sarbanes-Oxley Act of 2002 (SOX), the Gramm-Leach-Bliley Act (GLBA), and the Payment Card Industry Data Security Standard (PCI DSS).

By centralizing the system logging service, a security officer can accumulate systems logs from hundreds of systems and look at patterns of unusual activity across those various VLANs and network segments. An additional benefit of central logging is that if a system is compromised, the log entries leading up to that compromise will be preserved. This can be very important when examining the cause of a security compromise and looking for other computers that might be affected. Clear policies and procedures regarding the capture, retention, and use of system logs are essential to protect the privacy of those using the systems.

The National Institute of Standards and Technology (NIST) recommends the following areas be established and practiced:

- Prioritize log management appropriately throughout the organization.
- Create and maintain a log management infrastructure.
- Provide proper support for all staff with log management responsibilities.
- Establish standard log management operational processes.

Below is a listing of valuable resources to establish and define your logging content and requirements:

ORGANIZATION	URL
CERT® Coordination Center (CERT/CC)	http://www.cert.org/
Cryptographic Module Validation Program (CMVP)	http://csrc.nist.gov/cryptval/
IETF Extended Incident Handling Working Group	http://www.ietf.org/html.charters/inch-charter.html
IETF Security Issues in Network Event Logging Working Group	http://www.ietf.org/html.charters/syslog-charter.html
IETF Syslog Working Group	http://www.employees.org/~lonvick/index.shtml
LogAnalysis mailing list archive	http://lists.shmoo.com/mailman/listinfo/loganalysis
LogAnalysis.org	http://www.loganalysis.org/
LogBlog	http://blog.loglogic.com/
SANS Institute	http://www.sans.org/
SANS Institute log analysis mailing list archive	http://lists.sans.org/mailman/listinfo/log-analysis
SANS Institute webcast archive	http://www.sans.org/webcasts/archive.php
Syslog.org	http://www.syslog.org/
Talisker Security Wizardry Portal	http://www.networkintrusion.co.uk/
Unofficial Log Parser support site	http://www.logparser.com/
U.S. Computer Emergency Readiness Team (US-CERT)	http://www.us-cert.gov/

Clients are one of the targets; securing the client computers using sound industry practices and a level of client/host-based security is an important part of our IT security architecture. The Defense Information Security Agency has many Security Technical Implementation Guides (STIGs) that are a valuable resource for the client, as well as every other device on the network. Using the STIGs and NIST in conjunction will make your job easier and also assist in creating the policies needed to document your procedures.

Server-Side Security

In many, if not all, organizations the infrastructure is divided into multiple areas; these areas include the servers. As discussed within the client-side security, many of these steps include each of the previous eight steps. Of the eight steps, steps 1, 5, 6, 7, and 8 also apply to the server-side security. Of these, steps 6, 7, and 8 are the most critical in protecting your infrastructure. We could list the number and types of servers your infrastructure needs, but that would be subjective to your actual infrastructure. Instead, let's look at what kinds of servers you have to support your client/host systems:

- Domain controllers
- Secondary domain controllers
- Intra/extranet authentication servers
- Email servers
- Database servers
- File servers
- Portal servers
- Log servers
- Virtual servers
- Single sign-on servers
- Web servers

Although each of these poses a different level of risk to the enterprise, each must be taken from the base load and secured in accordance to its purpose. Of these, a database server could pose the biggest threat, especially when coupled with a web server. Listed below are the most common vulnerabilities that pose the biggest threat to servers:

1. Default services
2. Lack of auditing
3. Misconfigured security controls
4. Excessive user rights
5. Misconfigured organizational units
6. Improper configuration management, change control

Understanding the proper configuration goals of the organization, its security model, and motivators will assist a good IT manager in the configuration of the organizational systems to meet the business needs. Following sound industry standards is essential in obtaining a secure foundation.

Strategy vs. Business Model

The successful alignment of security controls with business objectives requires a full understanding of the organization's:

- Business goals
- Mission statement

- Technologies in place and planned
- Capacity management procedures and metrics
- Security controls in place and planned
- Level of importance for security

Developing a comprehensive security architecture is a critical success factor in any organizational structure. Security architectures provide a scalable framework for integrating people, process, and technology-related controls that address both current and planned business objectives.

The security architecture model will provide the core infrastructure that supports the company's strategic business vision. Unlike other models, the security model defines the other processes—asset management, financial management, configuration management, change management, and so forth—by products. This model further serves as the substance for the security architecture model that includes detailed technical designs, product selection, development, implementation, support, as well as the ongoing management of an information system and technology infrastructure.

The relationship of information technology (IT) to the business must be well understood in order to properly align the security architecture model with critical business processes. Gaining this understanding will enable the security architecture model to be more focused on issues of prominence to the business model and mission, and concentrate security activities within those areas. Using the security architecture model will significantly enhance the architecture credibility as a well-rounded configuration that incorporates the technology, security, and integrity of that technology to achieve the business objectives that are focused on the organization. With regard to the security architecture model, this is critical to the model's ability to link the management, operational, and technical families within security and make recommendations for improvement to specific business needs and values, therefore enhancing the overall mission focus.

The value of the right technology to an organization is based upon the role it plays and can be categorized into five definitive groupings:

1. Achievement of business strategy coupled with mission
2. Leveraging of policy, procedures, and implementation into human knowledge

3. Promotion of operational efficiency and effectiveness
4. Facilitation of operational control and flexibility in periods of rapid change
5. Continuous monitoring of the assets and configurations

Understanding the business will help you develop a business risk framework of references for the logical assessment of IT security effectiveness and the development of strategies for the improvement of a highly relevant and changing organization. Components of the security architecture model must address the business risks, probability of occurrence, and ability to relate any security vulnerabilities to the business risks in order for the controls to be effective and the application of due care and due diligence meaningful and purposeful.

When you approach the key objectives of understanding the business model, you should take into consideration the following four objectives:

1. Identify the most important business processes and their boundaries within the infrastructure and within the organization to ensure that the security architecture model and improvement strategy efforts are focused on areas that support security, the risk framework, and the mission.
2. Understand the nature and extent of the business model and the dependency of key business enclaves, processes, and people to understand the importance of the entire system's role in the organization.
3. Gain an understanding of the business mission, business model, and information technology strategies, along with the users, to determine the impact of possible risks and future changes or upgrades and the importance of information technology's role within the organization and appropriate security architecture model as applied through the management, operational, and technical families of security controls.
4. Identify the nature and importance of information technology's role in the organization and the importance of data, data classification, and systems integrity within the organization.

Security Risk Framework

A successful IT risk management program is more than a simple checklist of do's and don'ts and a handful of policies and procedures. It is a proactive, ongoing program of identifying and assessing risk, and weighing business trade-offs on acceptable levels of risk against ever-changing technologies and solutions.

Extensive documentation is available on IT risk management and conducting IT self-assessments. It is recommended that IT organizations that support the electric infrastructure avail themselves of this documentation in developing their own risk management program to address the following key elements:

- System characterization
- Threat identification
- Vulnerability identification
- Security control analysis
- Likelihood determination
- Impact analysis
- Risk determination
- Control recommendation
- Results documentation

Risk assessment should consider the threat, system characteristics, and physical and cyber environments in which those systems operate.

This area is covered more in depth in Chapter 6, but the key points will be covered here to maintain continuity. Risk framing establishes the context and provides a common perspective on how organizations manage risk. Risk management framing, as its principal output, produces a risk management strategy that addresses how organizations intend to assess and mitigate each specific risk, and what steps are needed to monitor risk. The risk management framework requires specific disciplines, constraints, risk tolerances, and priorities used within organizations for making business risk decisions. The risk management strategy includes any strategic-level decisions and considerations on how risk to organizational operations and assets, individuals, other organizations, and the nation is to be managed by the organization. In order to adequately understand and apply the risks to the business model, you need to understand the security architecture of the business model and how it will be supported from a management perspective. You may need to step out and challenge management. During this phase, the initial questions should address the scope of the project from an information architecture perspective and should answer the following questions:

- What is the objective? Is it a process that is internally or externally developed?
- If there are multiple processes, are they interrelated or stand-alone? Will they rely on the same data, or the same functions, or are they functionally independent?
- Does the organization have the capacity and bandwidth (capacity management)?
- Are the processes existing ones that are used on an internal portal application, or are they being developed for public viewing?

A corporate challenge for many internal audit departments is auditing risk management. The following thoughts need to be considered when performing an assessment:

- The risk of poor risk management
- What metrics we use to audit risk management and whether there is a gap analysis
- Why we need risk management and what value it should provide
- A review of the major risk management standards/frameworks
- Suggested evaluation steps
- Risk management maturity
- Reporting

The output of the risk framing step is the risk management strategy that identifies how organizations intend to assess, respond to, and monitor risk over time. The framing step also produces a set of organizational policies, procedures, standards, guidance, and resources covering the following topics:

1. Scope of the organizational risk management process (e.g., organizational entities covered, mission/business functions affected, and how risk management activities are applied within the risk management tiers)

2. Risk assessment guidance, including, for example, the characterization of threat sources, sources of threat information, representative threat events (in particular, adversary tactics, techniques, and procedures), when to consider and how to evaluate threats, sources of vulnerability information, risk assessment methodologies to be used, and risk assumptions
3. Risk response guidance, including, for example, risk tolerances, risk response concepts to be employed, opportunity costs, trade-offs, consequences of responses, hierarchy of authorities, and priorities
4. Risk monitoring guidance, including, for example, guidance on analysis of monitored risk factors to determine changes in risk, and monitoring frequency, methods, and reporting
5. Other risk constraints on executing risk management activities
6. Organizational priorities and trade-offs; outputs from the risk framing step serve as inputs to the risk assessment, risk response, and risk monitoring steps

Now that the functional requirements of business process are better understood and the supporting technical specifications (unique information architecture and the technology infrastructure that is required to support it) have been identified, an assessment of the relative risk can be conducted. The risk can be evaluated at a specific technology component level (operating system, network component, application, database, code, etc.) or ultimately at the residual risk level.

Once the project team has identified and understands the associated risks, a comparison of the risks against the existing security architecture is required to identify potential control gaps. The gap analysis, capacity, and controls assessment also serve as an opportunity to revalidate the effectiveness of the existing security architecture in supporting the continued business needs of the organization. When a gap is identified, as a result of a new requirement, technology vulnerability, etc., the analysis team should develop a plan of actions and milestones (POA&M) that includes a cost–benefit analysis and, as a minimum:

- Threat assessment
- Business process
- Residual risk determination
- Controls assessment

- Vulnerability assessment
- Risk management process

The development, integration, and implementation of the seven phases should be followed, and should include an emphasis on building secure applications. Training classes for application developers are often a good idea, especially if the in-house staff is unfamiliar with web-based authentication methods, cryptography tools, and general secure coding practices. Preproduction testing should focus on security as well as functionality, perhaps through the use of in-house or external vulnerability assessment teams. In some companies, an internal audit may also be involved in this phase.

The overall plan should be presented to the stakeholders so they recognize the risk, and a strategy should be developed to accept, avoid, transfer, mitigate, or even ignore the results.

1. **Risk acceptance:** Acceptance is often taken as a risk strategy in the prediction and mitigation process. Risk acceptance would only be applied to low-priority risks.
   a. Passive risk acceptance is accepting the risk.
   b. Active risk acceptance is developing a mitigation plan to accommodate apparent and actual threats.
2. **Risk avoidance:** Risk avoidance involves modifying the overall project management plan to mitigate the threat. Risks that are identified can be mitigated by identifying the following:
   a. The level of threat.
   b. The possibility of the threat agent becoming active.
   c. The probability of the threat agent becoming active (quantitative).
      - The annualized loss expectancy (ALE) is a monetary loss that can be expected for a system due to a risk over a one-year period. It is defined as

      $$ALE = SLE * ARO$$

      where SLE is the single loss expectancy and ARO is the annualized rate of occurrence.
3. **Risk transfer:** Risk transfer shifts the impact of a threat to a third party. Risk transfer does not eliminate a threat; it simply makes another party responsible for managing it.

4. **Risk mitigation:** Risk mitigation involves reducing the probability and impact of threat to an acceptable level. Taking a proactive approach against a risk is often more effective than a reactive approach. A well-developed incident response plan can be active and also reactive. Although we cannot predict what is going to happen, we can be prepared for the common threats that our systems are exposed to and have "something" in place to deter the affects.

5. **Ignore risk:** Ignoring risk is an option, not a sound one, but one that transfers the responsibility to the stakeholders and makes the organization liable. The level of liability depends on the level of risk and if the threat agent is probable.

An integrated risk management program is critical in securing business objectives requiring the enforcement of confidentiality, integrity, availability, accountability, and access.

The most important aspects of any security architecture model are the ability to manage, implement, sustain, and monitor an accurate and consistent level of security controls. Many organizations have data and data centers. Some of the many questions you need to ask are

1. What are the systems, and what are they used for?
2. What type of data is being processed, stored, and used?
3. Who is the data owner?
4. What interconnections are in place, and are they ad hoc, authorized, and documented?
5. What is being done to test the level of security on each system?
6. What is being done to test the level of security and configuration of the databases?

As you will see from the following list, portfolio management process takes into account many aspects of enterprise security architecture and also leads into the various chapters of this book. As with any architecture, your management process is essential and must be repeatable to obtain a systematic view and approach to your infrastructure security.

- *Identification* of assets, people, dollars, and interconnections
- *Categorization* of each system, each risk factor, and position
- *Evaluation* of your infrastructure, their projects, and people

- *Selection* of the best approach to management of projects, people, and things
- *Prioritization* of your projects, dollars, and timelines
- *Balance* your time, assets, bandwidth, and budget
- *Authorization* to perform your functions, delegation of functions, and decision making
- *Review and report* to all stakeholders and subordinates
- *Strategic change* implementation, tracking, and monitoring

Once you have reached out and "discovered" your infrastructure, you can logically move forward and develop and categorize your systems to be more effective in your organization. By more effective, I mean functionally within the security model, having the ability to determine your boundaries, business functions, shared resources, interconnections, etc.

With input from the enterprise security division, the stakeholders establish security categories for both information and information systems. The security categories are based on the potential impact on an organization and, should certain events occur that threaten the information and information systems needed by the organization to accomplish its assigned mission, protect its assets, fulfill its legal responsibilities, maintain its day-to-day functions, and protect individuals. Security categories should be used in conjunction with vulnerability and threat information in assessing the risk to an organization.

4

SYSTEMS SECURITY CATEGORIZATION

Why do we categorize systems? One way to look at system categorization is to first understand the management aspect of an enterprise computing environment. Portfolio managers need a way to

1. Identify their assets.
2. Understand their assets' capabilities.
3. Understand their assets' configuration.
4. Define and understand interconnections, either internal or external (partners).
5. Identify asset managers.
6. Identify their assets' interrelation with other assets.

The primary focus of this chapter is the internalization of the ongoing enterprise capability to make and implement portfolio management and risk management decisions in a consistent and disciplined manner by defining the system security categorization (SC) process and to provide you with a systematic way of placing your information technology assets into boundaries that are based upon the business and management functions of the organization. I like the National Institute of Standards and Technology (NIST) because it understands and builds your enterprise using security as the model. I have modified its way to expand on the requirements and also dig deeper into the process of building your enterprise using the security model of NIST. This modified NIST format, as shown below, is used to categorize each system and then develop logical business unit boundaries.

SC information type = {(**confidentiality**, *impact*), (**integrity**, *impact*), (**availability**, *impact*), (**access**, *impact*)}

When you start your system security categorization, it makes it easier for the stakeholders to understand the parts and pieces if you use categories that are easy to understand. Within the NIST, there are three categories that most people have become familiar with

1. General support system (GSS)
2. Major application
3. Minor application

General support system: An interconnected information resource under the same direct management control that shares common functionality. It normally includes hardware, software, information, data, applications, communications, facilities, and people and provides support for a variety of users and applications. Individual applications support different mission-related functions. Users may be from the same or different organizations.

Major application: An application that requires special attention to security due to the risk and magnitude of the harm resulting from the loss, misuse, or unauthorized access to or modification of the information in the application. A breach in a major application might comprise many individual application programs and hardware, software, and telecommunications components. Major applications can be either a major software application or a combination of hardware and software where the only purpose of the system is to support a specific mission-related function.

Minor application: An application, other than a major application, that requires attention to security due to the risk and magnitude of harm resulting from the loss, misuse, or unauthorized access to or modification of the information in the application. Minor applications are typically included as part of a general support system and rely on the GSS for all or most of their security.

System security categorization is one of the most difficult tasks facing a policy and procedure manager when establishing security categories for both information and information systems. In an attempt to relieve the agony in developing a system security categorization structure, I have tried simplifying it; for starters, it is a good idea to base the security categories of the information system on the potential impact on the business model of the "division" of your organization. As shown below, the identity access management (IAM) portion of the infrastructure has been bordered in red to show that that portion of the infrastructure is under one level of management and defines one major application in the scheme of the enterprise. Although the IAM touches many aspects of the enterprise infrastructure, it has been sectioned out within that structure and given to a specific manager to ensure that the major application is managed, up to date, and documented. When writing about the IAM infrastructure, you may mention interconnections, agreements, trusted sources, network segments, and so forth; regardless, document the entire infrastructure. Example document templates have been provided in the appendixes of this book under the system security plan (SSP) folder (Figure 4.1).

So, you have many separate network segments that cross many borders. Who's in charge? Who manages it? Who commits it to change? Good questions. This will be something that is suggested by careful collaboration between the network and systems managers, the chief information officer (CIO), the chief technology officer (CTO), or maybe the chief information security officer (CISO),

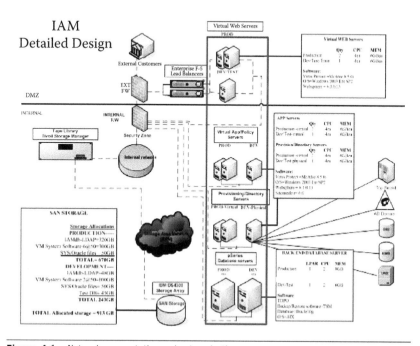

Figure 4.1   Network segmentation and categorization.

depending on how your organization is segmented or partitioned. Regardless, however it is defined, segmenting is a good way to maintain control, and segmenting by management unit promotes ownership and may enhance your level of security when a manager has "ownership" of the systems the department uses. Although it will be a shared responsibility between the information technology specialists for administration, the department manager should know his or her applications and databases and who needs what level of access. Management doesn't necessarily mean ownership but "ownership" is the shifting of responsibilities and accountability of the system so there is a "go-to guy" for answers! All systems should be monitored by specific personnel that specialize in the functions of monitoring and also for the software updates. When certain events occur that jeopardize the information and information systems needed by the organization to accomplish its assigned mission, protect its assets, maintain its day-to-day functions, and protect individuals, the major aspects of the security architecture are understood and defined, whereas the security cell can respond and have a manager that understands its systems and any specific upgrade or access projects taking place. Security categories are to be used in conjunction with vulnerability and threat information in assessing the risk to an organization.

To further the process a manager needs to develop some definitions of categories for the information and the information systems. The NIST has defined data in three separate areas; an additional area has been added that aids in the control of data:

1. **CONFIDENTIALITY**—Preserving authorized restrictions on information access and disclosure, including means for protecting personal privacy and proprietary information. (44 U.S.C., Sec. 3542)

   A loss of confidentiality is the unauthorized disclosure of information.

2. **INTEGRITY**—Guarding against improper information modification or destruction, and includes ensuring information non-repudiation and authenticity. (44 U.S.C., Sec. 3542)

   A loss of integrity is the unauthorized modification or destruction of information.

3. **AVAILABILITY**—Ensuring timely and reliable access to and use of information. (44 U.S.C., Sec. 3542)

A loss of availability is the disruption of access to or use of information or an information system.

4. **ACCESS**—The authorization and rights you have to access or not to access data that are related to storing, retrieving, or acting on data housed in a database or other source.

The application of these definitions must take place within the context of each organization and the overall organizational stakeholder's interest.

Within the NIST's model, systems are labeled by the importance to the organization and the impact the systems have on that organization. For example, a financial system database would pose more of a threat to the business functions vs. a database that maintains training attendance—one spectrum to the other, but a definitive difference of the types of data stored. In this example you might have a high vs. moderate CIAA (confidentiality, integrity, availability, and access) using the example formula.

SC information type = {(**confidentiality**, *impact*), (**integrity**, *impact*), (**availability**, *impact*), (**access**, *impact*)}

Financial system = {(**confidentiality**, *high*), (**integrity**, *high*), (**availability**, *moderate*), **access**, *high*)}

Training data = {(**confidentiality**, *moderate*), (**integrity**, *low*), (**availability**, *low*), (**access**, *low*)}

Because the confidentiality of the personnel data might be moderate, due to the amount of personal information you obtain, this could be low if it is just the person's employee number. When any one of the three categories is a higher category than the others, it would inherit the cover of the highest system security category available.

Now, this is also to say that when you select your security controls using NIST SP 800-53, you would need to select the proper security controls that pertain to the moderate confidentiality control families.

When selecting your security controls NIST SP 800-53 states the "high-water mark" is what is used across the board; this is costly and may be prohibitive to an organization in completing an initial objective of data or system security. Although it is a good practice to follow the guidelines, the final determination will come from the stakeholders and information security personnel. Following the guidance will help establish an initial baseline, and as your risk evaluation ages and you become more familiar with the process, a customized set of controls may be applied.

What about a human resources database of employees' information, social security numbers, home addresses, phone numbers, corporate position risk, and work location over the organization's financial data? Although you have two very important data stores of information, are they both rated high?

To give clearer understandings of how to implement the system security categorization, follow these guidelines:

The potential impact is low if

SC information type = {(confidentiality, low), (integrity, low), (availability, low), (access, low)}

The loss of confidentiality, integrity, availability, or access could be expected to have a limited adverse effect on organizational operations, organizational assets, or individuals.

Amplification: A limited adverse effect means that, for example, the loss of confidentiality, integrity, availability, or access might

1. Cause a degradation in mission capability to an extent and duration that the organization is able to perform its primary functions, but the effectiveness of the functions is noticeably reduced
2. Result in minor damage to organizational assets
3. Result in minor financial loss
4. Result in minor harm to individuals
5. Cause login capabilities to be restricted in time

The potential impact is moderate if

SC information type = {(confidentiality, moderate), (integrity, moderate), (availability, moderate), (access, moderate)}

The loss of confidentiality, integrity, availability, or access could be expected to have a serious adverse effect on organizational operations, organizational assets, or individuals.

Amplification: A serious adverse effect means that, for example, the loss of confidentiality, integrity, availability, or access might

1. Cause a significant degradation in mission capability to an extent and duration that the organization is able to perform its primary functions, but the effectiveness of the functions is significantly reduced
2. Result in significant damage to organizational assets
3. Result in significant financial loss
4. Result in significant harm to an individual that does not involve loss of life or serious life-threatening injuries
5. Cause login to be determined as malicious, data breach to be limited, or login to be restricted to an undetermined amount of time

The potential impact is high if

SC information type = {(confidentiality, high), (integrity, high), (availability, high), (access, high)}

The loss of confidentiality, integrity, availability, or access could be expected to have a severe or catastrophic adverse effect on organizational operations, organizational assets, or individuals.

Amplification: A severe or catastrophic adverse effect means that, for example, the loss of confidentiality, integrity, availability, or access might

1. Cause a severe degradation in or loss of mission capability to an extent and duration that the organization is not able to perform one or more of its primary functions
2. Result in major damage to organizational assets
3. Result in major financial loss
4. Result in severe or catastrophic harm to individuals involving loss of life or serious life-threatening injuries

5. Cause access to be malicious, data to be breached, and the probability of identity theft to be extreme

When reviewing the security controls applied to a particular information system, the security manager and stakeholders should determine that the controls applied must be proportionate with the potential impact on the organization's operations, assets, individuals, interconnections, and the overall business model in the event there is a loss of confidentiality, integrity, availability, or access.

When selecting your controls to apply to a specific system or enclave, select the level of controls that meet or exceed the area your concern is in. For example, as discussed previously' the confidentiality was moderate but the integrity and availability were low on the training system. Therefore, you would select system security controls that apply to the low side of availability and integrity and moderate controls that deal with protecting confidentiality. Within the appendix a Microsoft Excel spreadsheet has been provided on the CRC Press website to assist in selection and evaluation of the controls. Table 4.1 shows 18 control families from NIST SP 800-53, revision 3.

System Security Categorization Applied to Information Types

The security category of an information type can be associated with both user information and system information and can be applicable to information in either electronic or nonelectronic form (soft or hard copy). The user and system information can also be used as input in considering the appropriate security category of an information system. Establishing an appropriate security category of an information type essentially requires determining the potential impact for each security objective associated with the particular information type. In selection of the controls look at the entire enterprise and never reduce your level of controls; if they need moderate, do not apply low due to costs, when cost is not a driving factor. Keep in mind the regulations that your organizations must adhere to for compliance—your decision could cost the business hundreds, if not thousands, of dollars, just to save a few bucks!

Table 4.2 will aid you in determining the level of impact that an event may have and the consequences on your system or organization.

Table 4.1   Control Families from NIST SP 800-53, Revision 3

CONTROL NO.	CONTROL NAME	CONTROL BASELINES		
		LOW	MODERATE	HIGH
ACCESS CONTROL				
AC-1	Access Control Policy and Procedures	AC-1	AC-1	AC-1
AC-2	Account Management	AC-2	AC-2 (1) (2) (3) (4) (5) (6)	AC-2 (1) (2) (3) (4) (5) (6)
AC-3	Access Enforcement	AC-3	AC-3	AC-3
AC-4	Information Flow Enforcement	Not selected	AC-4	AC-4
AC-5	Separation of Duties	Not selected	AC-5	AC-5
AC-6	Least Privilege	Not selected	AC-6 (1) (2)	AC-6 (1) (2)
AC-7	Unsuccessful Login Attempts	AC-7	AC-7	AC-7
AC-8	System Use Notification	AC-8	AC-8	AC-8
AC-9	Previous Logon Notification	Not selected	Not selected	Not selected
AC-10	Concurrent Session Control	Not selected	Not selected	AC-10
AC-11	Session Lock	Not selected	AC-11	AC-11
AC-12	Session Termination (Withdrawn)	—	—	—
AC-13	Supervision and Review—Access Control (Withdrawn)	—	—	—
AC-14	Permitted Actions without Identification or Authentication	AC-14	AC-14 (1)	AC-14 (1)
AC-15	Automated Marking (Withdrawn)	—	—	—
AC-16	Automated Labeling	Not selected	Not selected	Not selected
AC-17	Remote Access	AC-17	AC-17 (1) (2) (3) (4) (5)	AC-17 (1) (2) (3) (4) (5) (6)
AC-18	Wireless Access Restrictions (Withdrawn)	—	—	—
AC-19	Access Control for Mobile Devices	AC-19	AC-19 (1) (2) (3)	AC-19 (1) (2) (3)
AC-20	Use of External Information Systems	AC-20	AC-20 (1) (2)	AC-20 (1) (2)
AC-21	User-Based Collaboration and Information Sharing	Not selected	Not selected	Not selected
AWARENESS AND TRAINING				
AT-1	Security Awareness and Training Policy and Procedures	AT-1	AT-1	AT-1
AT-2	Security Awareness	AT-2	AT-2	AT-2
AT-3	Security Training	AT-3	AT-3	AT-3

(*Continued*)

Table 4.1 (*Continued*) Control Families from NIST SP 800-53, Revision 3

CONTROL NO.	CONTROL NAME	CONTROL BASELINES		
		LOW	MODERATE	HIGH
AT-4	Security Training Records	AT-4	AT-4	AT-4
AT-5	Contacts with Security Groups and Associations	Not Selected	Not Selected	Not Selected
AUDIT AND ACCOUNTABILITY				
AU-1	Audit and Accountability Policy and Procedures	AU-1	AU-1	AU-1
AU-2	Auditable Events	AU-2	AU-2 (3) (4)	AU-2 (3) (4)
AU-3	Content of Audit Records	AU-3	AU-3 (1)	AU-3 (1) (2)
AU-4	Audit Storage Capacity	AU-4	AU-4	AU-4
AU-5	Response to Audit Processing Failures	AU-5	AU-5	AU-5 (1) (2)
AU-6	Audit Review, Analysis, and Reporting	Not selected	AU-6	AU-6 (1)
AU-7	Audit Reduction and Report Generation	Not selected	AU-7 (1)	AU-7 (1)
AU-8	Time Stamps	AU-8	AU-8 (1)	AU-8 (1)
AU-9	Protection of Audit Information	AU-9	AU-9	AU-9
AU-10	Nonrepudiation	Not selected	Not selected	Not selected
AU-11	Audit Record Retention	AU-11	AU-11	AU-11
AU-12	Audit Generation	AU-12	AU-12	AU-12 (1)
SECURITY ASSESSMENT AND AUTHORIZATION				
CA-1	Security Assessment and Authorization Policies and Procedures	CA-1	CA-1	CA-1
CA-2	Security Assessments	CA-2	CA-2 (1)	CA-2 (1)
CA-3	Information System Connections	CA-3	CA-3	CA-3
CA-4	Security Certification (Withdrawn)	—	—	—
CA-5	Plan of Action and Milestones	CA-5	CA-5	CA-5
CA-6	Security Authorization	CA-6	CA-6	CA-6
CA-7	Continuous Monitoring	CA-7	CA-7	CA-7
CONFIGURATION MANAGEMENT				
CM-1	Configuration Management Policy and Procedures	CM-1	CM-1	CM-1
CM-2	Baseline Configuration	CM-2	CM-2 (1)	CM-2 (1) (2) (3) (4)
CM-3	Configuration Change Control	Not selected	CM-3 (2)	CM-3 (1) (2)
CM-4	Security Impact Analysis	Not selected	CM-4	CM-4
CM-5	Access Restrictions for Change	Not selected	CM-5	CM-5 (1) (2) (3)

Table 4.1 (*Continued*)   Control Families from NIST SP 800-53, Revision 3

CONTROL NO.	CONTROL NAME	CONTROL BASELINES		
		LOW	MODERATE	HIGH
CM-6	Configuration Settings	CM-6	CM-6	CM-6 (1) (2)
CM-7	Least Functionality	Not selected	CM-7 (1)	CM-7 (1) (2)
CM-8	Information System Component Inventory	CM-8	CM-8 (1)	CM-8 (1) (2) (3) (4)
CM-9	Configuration Management Plan	Not selected	Not selected	Not selected
CONTINGENCY PLANNING				
CP-1	Contingency Planning Policy and Procedures	CP-1	CP-1	CP-1
CP-2	Contingency Plan	CP-2	CP-2 (1)	CP-2 (1) (2) (3)
CP-3	Contingency Training	CP-3	CP-3	CP-3 (1)
CP-4	Contingency Plan Testing and Exercises	CP-4	CP-4 (1)	CP-4 (1) (2) (4)
CP-5	Contingency Plan Update (Withdrawn)	—	—	—
CP-6	Alternate Storage Site	Not selected	CP-6 (1) (3)	CP-6 (1) (2) (3)
CP-7	Alternate Processing Site	Not selected	CP-7 (1) (2) (3) (5)	CP-7 (1) (2) (3) (4) (5)
CP-8	Telecommunications Services	Not selected	CP-8 (1) (2)	CP-8 (1) (2) (3) (4)
CP-9	Information System Backup	CP-9	CP-9 (1)	CP-9 (1) (2) (3)
CP-10	Information System Recovery and Reconstitution	CP-10	CP-10	CP-10 (3) (4)
IDENTIFICATION AND AUTHENTICATION				
IA-1	Identification and Authentication Policy and Procedures	IA-1	IA-1	IA-1
IA-2	Identification and Authentication (Organizational Users)	IA-2	IA-2 (1)	IA-2 (1)
IA-3	Device Identification and Authentication	Not selected	IA-3	IA-3
IA-4	Identifier Management	IA-4	IA-4	IA-4
IA-5	Authenticator Management	IA-5	IA-5 (1)	IA-5 (1)
IA-6	Authenticator Feedback	IA-6	IA-6	IA-6
IA-7	Cryptographic Module Authentication	IA-7	IA-7	IA-7
IA-8	Identification and Authentication (Nonorganizational Users)	IA-8	IA-8	IA-8

(*Continued*)

Table 4.1 (*Continued*)   Control Families from NIST SP 800-53, Revision 3

CONTROL NO.	CONTROL NAME	CONTROL BASELINES		
		LOW	MODERATE	HIGH
INCIDENT RESPONSE				
IR-1	Incident Response Policy and Procedures	IR-1	IR-1	IR-1
IR-2	Incident Response Training	Not selected	IR-2	IR-2 (1)
IR-3	Incident Response Testing and Exercises	Not selected	IR-3	IR-3 (1)
IR-4	Incident Handling	IR-4	IR-4 (1)	IR-4 (1)
IR-5	Incident Monitoring	Not selected	IR-5	IR-5 (1)
IR-6	Incident Reporting	IR-6	IR-6 (1)	IR-6 (1)
IR-7	Incident Response Assistance	IR-7	IR-7 (1)	IR-7 (1)
MAINTENANCE				
MA-1	System Maintenance Policy and Procedures	MA-1	MA-1	MA-1
MA-2	Controlled Maintenance	MA-2	MA-2 (1)	MA-2 (1) (2)
MA-3	Maintenance Tools	Not selected	MA-3	MA-3 (1) (2) (3)
MA-4	Remote Maintenance	MA-4	MA-4 (1) (2)	MA-4 (1) (2) (3)
MA-5	Maintenance Personnel	MA-5	MA-5	MA-5
MA-6	Timely Maintenance	Not selected	MA-6	MA-6
MEDIA PROTECTION				
MP-1	Media Protection Policy and Procedures	MP-1	MP-1	MP-1
MP-2	Media Access	MP-2	MP-2 (1)	MP-2 (1)
MP-3	Media Marking	Not selected	Not selected	MP-3 (1)
MP-4	Media Storage	Not selected	MP-4	MP-4
MP-5	Media Transport	Not selected	MP-5 (2)	MP-5 (2) (3)
MP-6	Media Sanitization	MP-6	MP-6	MP-6 (1) (2)
PHYSICAL AND ENVIRONMENTAL PROTECTION				
PE-1	Physical and Environmental Protection Policy and Procedures	PE-1	PE-1	PE-1
PE-2	Physical Access Authorizations	PE-2	PE-2	PE-2
PE-3	Physical Access Control	PE-3	PE-3	PE-3 (1)
PE-4	Access Control for Transmission Medium	Not selected	Not selected	PE-4
PE-5	Access Control for Display Medium	Not selected	PE-5	PE-5
PE-6	Monitoring Physical Access	PE-6	PE-6 (1)	PE-6 (1) (2)
PE-7	Visitor Control	PE-7	PE-7 (1)	PE-7 (1)

Table 4.1 (*Continued*) Control Families from NIST SP 800-53, Revision 3

CONTROL NO.	CONTROL NAME	CONTROL BASELINES		
		LOW	MODERATE	HIGH
PE-8	Access Records	PE-8	PE-8	PE-8 (1) (2)
PE-9	Power Equipment and Power Cabling	Not selected	PE-9	PE-9
PE-10	Emergency Shutoff	Not selected	PE-10	PE-10
PE-11	Emergency Power	Not selected	PE-11	PE-11 (1)
PE-12	Emergency Lighting	PE-12	PE-12	PE-12
PE-13	Fire Protection	PE-13	PE-13 (1) (2) (3)	PE-13 (1) (2) (3)
PE-14	Temperature and Humidity Controls	PE-14	PE-14	PE-14
PE-15	Water Damage Protection	PE-15	PE-15	PE-15 (1)
PE-16	Delivery and Removal	PE-16	PE-16	PE-16
PE-17	Alternate Work Site	Not selected	PE-17	PE-17
PE-18	Location of Information System Components	Not selected	PE-18	PE-18 (1)
PE-19	Information Leakage	Not selected	Not selected	Not selected
PLANNING				
PL-1	Security Planning Policy and Procedures	PL-1	PL-1	PL-1
PL-2	System Security Plan	PL-2	PL-2	PL-2
PL-3	System Security Plan Update (Withdrawn)	—	—	—
PL-4	Rules of Behavior	PL-4	PL-4	PL-4
PL-5	Privacy Impact Assessment	PL-5	PL-5	PL-5
PL-6	Security-Related Activity Planning	Not selected	PL-6	PL-6
PERSONNEL SECURITY				
PS-1	Personnel Security Policy and Procedures	PS-1	PS-1	PS-1
PS-2	Position Categorization	PS-2	PS-2	PS-2
PS-3	Personnel Screening	PS-3	PS-3	PS-3
PS-4	Personnel Termination	PS-4	PS-4	PS-4
PS-5	Personnel Transfer	PS-5	PS-5	PS-5
PS-6	Access Agreements	PS-6	PS-6	PS-6
PS-7	Third-Party Personnel Security	PS-7	PS-7	PS-7
PS-8	Personnel Sanctions	PS-8	PS-8	PS-8

(*Continued*)

Table 4.1 (*Continued*)   Control Families from NIST SP 800-53, Revision 3

CONTROL NO.	CONTROL NAME	CONTROL BASELINES		
		LOW	MODERATE	HIGH
RISK ASSESSMENT				
RA-1	Risk Assessment Policy and Procedures	RA-1	RA-1	RA-1
RA-2	Security Categorization	RA-2	RA-2	RA-2
RA-3	Risk Assessment	RA-3	RA-3	RA-3
RA-4	Risk Assessment Update (Withdrawn)	—	—	—
RA-5	Vulnerability Scanning	RA-5	RA-5 (1)	RA-5 (1) (2) (3) (4) (5) (8)
SYSTEM AND SERVICES ACQUISITION				
SA-1	System and Services Acquisition Policy and Procedures	SA-1	SA-1	SA-1
SA-2	Allocation of Resources	SA-2	SA-2	SA-2
SA-3	Life Cycle Support	SA-3	SA-3	SA-3
SA-4	Acquisitions	SA-4	SA-4 (1)	SA-4 (1)
SA-5	Information System Documentation	SA-5	SA-5 (1) (3)	SA-5 (1) (2) (3)
SA-6	Software Usage Restrictions	SA-6	SA-6	SA-6
SA-7	User Installed Software	SA-7	SA-7	SA-7
SA-8	Security Engineering Principles	Not selected	SA-8	SA-8
SA-9	External Information System Services	SA-9	SA-9	SA-9
SA-10	Developer Configuration Management	Not selected	Not selected	SA-10
SA-11	Developer Security Testing	Not selected	SA-11	SA-11
SA-12	Supply Chain Protection	Not selected	Not selected	SA-12
SA-13	Trustworthiness	Not selected	Not selected	SA-13
SYSTEM AND COMMUNICATIONS PROTECTION				
SC-1	System and Communications Protection Policy and Procedures	SC-1	SC-1	SC-1
SC-2	Application Partitioning	Not selected	SC-2	SC-2
SC-3	Security Function Isolation	Not selected	Not selected	SC-3
SC-4	Information in Shared Resources	Not selected	SC-4	SC-4
SC-5	Denial of Service Protection	SC-5	SC-5	SC-5
SC-6	Resource Priority	Not selected	Not selected	Not selected
SC-7	Boundary Protection	SC-7	SC-7 (1) (2) (3) (4) (5) (10)	SC-7 (1) (2) (3) (4) (5) (6) (10) (11)

Table 4.1 (*Continued*)   Control Families from NIST SP 800-53, Revision 3

CONTROL NO.	CONTROL NAME	CONTROL BASELINES		
		LOW	MODERATE	HIGH
SC-8	Transmission Integrity	Not selected	SC-8 (1)	SC-8 (1)
SC-9	Transmission Confidentiality	Not selected	SC-9 (1)	SC-9 (1)
SC-10	Network Disconnect	Not selected	SC-10	SC-10
SC-11	Trusted Path	Not selected	Not selected	Not selected
SC-12	Cryptographic Key Establishment and Management	Not selected	SC-12	SC-12
SC-13	Use of Cryptography	SC-13	SC-13	SC-13
SC-14	Public Access Protections	SC-14	SC-14	SC-14
SC-15	Collaborative Computing Devices	Not selected	SC-15	SC-15
SC-16	Transmission of Security Parameters	Not selected	Not selected	Not selected
SC-17	Public Key Infrastructure Certificates	Not selected	SC-17	SC-17
SC-18	Mobile Code	Not selected	SC-18	SC-18
SC-19	Voice Over Internet Protocol	Not selected	SC-19	SC-19
SC-20	Secure Name/Address Resolution Service (Authoritative Source)	SC-20 (1)	SC-20 (1)	SC-20 (1)
SC-21	Secure Name/Address Resolution Service (Recursive or Caching Resolver)	Not selected	Not selected	SC-21
SC-22	Architecture and Provisioning for Name/Address Resolution Service	Not selected	SC-22	SC-22
SC-23	Session Authenticity	Not selected	SC-23	SC-23
SC-24	Fail in Known State	Not selected	Not selected	SC-24
SC-25	Thin Nodes	Not selected	Not selected	Not selected
SC-26	Honeypots	Not selected	Not selected	Not selected
SC-27	Operating System— Independent Applications	Not selected	Not selected	Not selected
SC-28	Confidentiality of Information at Rest	Not selected	SC-28	SC-28
SC-29	Heterogeneity	Not selected	Not selected	Not selected
SC-30	Abstraction Techniques	Not selected	Not selected	Not selected
SC-31	Covert Channel Analysis	Not selected	Not selected	Not selected

(*Continued*)

Table 4.1 (*Continued*)   Control Families from NIST SP 800-53, Revision 3

CONTROL NO.	CONTROL NAME	CONTROL BASELINES		
		LOW	MODERATE	HIGH
SYSTEM AND INFORMATION INTEGRITY				
SI-1	System and Information Integrity Policy and Procedures	SI-1	SI-1	SI-1
SI-2	Flaw Remediation	SI-2	SI-2 (2)	SI-2 (1) (2)
SI-3	Malicious Code Protection	SI-3	SI-3 (1) (2) (3)	SI-3 (1) (2) (3)
SI-4	Information System Monitoring	Not selected	SI-4 (2) (4) (5) (6)	SI-4 (2) (4) (5) (6)
SI-5	Security Alerts, Advisories, and Directives	SI-5	SI-5	SI-5 (1)
SI-6	Security Functionality Verification	Not selected	Not selected	SI-6
SI-7	Software and Information Integrity	Not selected	Not selected	SI-7 (1) (2)
SI-8	Spam Protection	Not selected	SI-8	SI-8 (1)
SI-9	Information Input Restrictions	Not selected	SI-9	SI-9
SI-10	Information Accuracy, Completeness, Validity, and Authenticity	Not selected	SI-10	SI-10
SI-11	Error Handling	Not selected	SI-11	SI-11
SI-12	Information Output Handling and Retention	Not selected	SI-12	SI-12
SI-13	Predictable Failure Prevention	Not selected	Not selected	Not selected
PROGRAM MANAGEMENT				
PM-1	Security Program Plan	P1		
PM-2	Senior Information Security Officer	P1		
PM-3	Information Security Resources	P1		
PM-4	Plan of Action and Milestones Process	P1		
PM-5	Information System Inventory	P1		
PM-6	Information Security Measures of Performance	P1	Deployed organization-wide Supporting all baselines	
PM-7	Enterprise Architecture	P1		
PM-8	Critical Infrastructure Plan	P1		
PM-9	Risk Management Strategy	P1		
PM-10	Security Authorization Process	P1		
PM-11	Mission/Business Process Definition	P1		

Table 4.2 Potential Impact

SECURITY OBJECTIVE	LOW	MODERATE	HIGH
CONFIDENTIALITY			
Preserving authorized restrictions on information access and disclosure, including means for protecting personal privacy and proprietary information (44 U.S.C., Sec. 3542)	The unauthorized disclosure of information could be expected to have a *limited* adverse effect on organizational operations, organizational assets, or individuals.	The unauthorized disclosure of information could be expected to have a *serious* adverse effect on organizational operations, organizational assets, or individuals.	The unauthorized disclosure of information could be expected to have a *severe or catastrophic* adverse effect on organizational operations, organizational assets, or individuals.
INTEGRITY			
Guarding against improper information modification or destruction; ensuring information nonrepudiation and authenticity (44 U.S.C., Sec. 3542)	The unauthorized modification or destruction of information could be expected to have a *limited* adverse effect on organizational operations, organizational assets, or individuals.	The unauthorized modification or destruction of information could be expected to have a *serious* adverse effect on organizational operations, organizational assets, or individuals.	The unauthorized modification or destruction of information could be expected to have a *severe or catastrophic* adverse effect on organizational operations, organizational assets, or individuals.
AVAILABILITY			
Ensuring timely and reliable access to and use of information (44 U.S.C., Sec. 3542)	The disruption of access to or use of information or an information system could be expected to have a *limited* adverse effect on organizational operations, organizational assets, or individuals.	The disruption of access to or use of information or an information system could be expected to have a *serious* adverse effect on organizational operations, organizational assets, or individuals.	The disruption of access to or use of information or an information system could be expected to have a *severe or catastrophic* adverse effect on organizational operations, organizational assets, or individuals.

Application of System Security Controls

The security control selection process described previously can be applied to organizational information systems from two different perspectives:

1. New development
2. Legacy or production systems

For a new development system, the security control selection process is applied from a requirements definition perspective since the information system does not yet exist and the organization is conducting an initial security categorization. The security controls included in the security plan for the information system serve as a security specification for the organization and are expected to be incorporated into the system during the development and implementation phases of the system development life cycle. The development phase of the new system is the birthplace for documenting the security controls you put or plan on putting in place for the system. Commercial vendors can assist you in documenting the controls if you have a specific application that resides on the system. The vendors are more than willing to provide you with trusted facility manuals (TFMs) for their software, and in the recent past have started to understand the requirements of the document. The TFM defines what security has been built in to the application or device, what range of ports the systems/devices within the network operate on, and other technical and security aspects of the application or device; you must ask for it or request it during the procurement process.

For a legacy or production information system, the security control selection process is applied from a gap analysis perspective. The gap analysis can be applied when the organization is anticipating significant changes to the system (e.g., during major upgrades, modifications, or outsourcing) or when the system is assigned new management, or existing management needs to include it into the portfolio management process. Since the information system already exists, the organization should have completed the security categorization and security control selection processes resulting in the documentation of a previously agreed upon set of security controls documented in the security plan and the implementation of those controls within the information system. Taking this into account, the gap analysis can be completed in the following manner:

1. Reconfirm the security categorization for the information and information system based on the different types of information that are currently processed, stored, or transmitted by the system. Update security categorization information, as necessary. Further guidance can be obtained from FIPS 199 and NIST Special Publications for guidance on security categorization.

2. Review the existing security plan, if it exists, for the information system that describes the security requirements and associated security controls that are currently employed and document in the plan any additional controls that would be needed by the system to ensure that the risk to organizational operations of the business, assets, individuals, and interconnections remains at an acceptable level. Additionally, if you do not have a documented system, now would be a good time to start one. A basic example has been included in the appendix material given on the CRC Press website.

3. Implement the security controls described in the updated security plan, document in the plan of action and milestone any security controls not implemented, and continue with the risk management framework in the same manner as a new development system.

The gap analysis perspective is also applied when interacting with external service providers, interconnections, and requests for new connections to ensure that a security posture exists within the information systems. Using the steps in the gap analysis described previously, the organization can effectively use the acquisition process and appropriate contractual vehicles to require external providers to carry out, in collaboration with the organization, the security categorization and security control selection steps in the risk management framework (RMF). The resulting information can help determine what security controls the external provider either has in place or intends to implement for the information system services that are to be provided to the organization. If a security control gap exists, the organization can reduce the organizational risk to an acceptable level by using the existing contractual vehicle to

- Require the external provider to meet the additional security control requirements established by the organization.
- If the existing contractual vehicle does not provide for such added requirements, negotiate with the provider for additional security controls (including compensating controls).
- Document the agreement within an interconnection agreement and point out the specifics of both parties and the exchange of a trusted facility manual (TFM) as part of the agreement.

Once you have identified your data, the system, and developed your categories, you should look at what controls need to be in place to protect those data and the IS. The minimum security requirements explained previously identify 18 different families and control types to apply toward your data and IS. Although not each of the controls may be required, you may have to establish a mixture of the controls to obtain your best coverage. In determining the category of a system, evaluate each of the areas of CIAA separately and apply controls that pertain to the data at the level you have determined to fit for the area.

Minimum Security Requirements

The minimum security requirements cover 18 system security-related areas with regard to protecting the confidentiality, integrity, availability, and access of information systems and the information processed, stored, and transmitted by those systems. The system security-related areas include the following:

1. Access control
2. Awareness and training
3. Audit and accountability
4. Certification, accreditation, and security assessments
5. Configuration management
6. Contingency planning

7. Identification and authentication
8. Incident response
9. Maintenance
10. Media protection
11. Physical and environmental protection
12. Planning
13. Personnel security
14. Risk assessment
15. Systems and services acquisition
16. System and communications protection
17. System and information integrity
18. Program management

The 18 areas represent a broad-based, balanced information security program that addresses the management, operational, and technical aspects of protecting your information and information systems. The Defense Information Systems Agency (DISA) provides Security Technical Implementation Guides (STIGs), and additionally, the National Security Agency (NSA) guides are the configuration standards for Department of Defense (DOD) information assurance (IA) and IA-enabled devices/systems. These guidelines will assist you in developing a complete, documented, security program that will adhere to any regulatory guidance to which your organization may be required to comply. The link to those STIGs is http://iase.disa.mil/stigs/a-z.html.

Policies and procedures play an important role in the effective implementation of enterprise-wide information security programs within the organization and the success of the resulting security measures employed to protect your information and information systems. Thus, organizations must develop and circulate formal, documented policies and procedures governing the minimum security requirements set forth in this standard and must ensure their effective implementation. The application of due diligence falls on the managers, but the ultimate responsibility falls upon the security personnel for advising the managers of industry best practices. Failing to do so will result in one of two options: you're fired or, worst yet, the data of the people that rely on you the most (users) will be out on the black market. The application of system security controls is a serious and sometimes unforgiving task that takes time and determination to apply what is needed without breaking functionality of an information system.

System Security Controls

Over the next few pages let's go over what the controls are and how they need to be applied by following what recommendations are listed. Although they state you *will* or *must* as a minimum, you should follow a strategic and directed method for complying with a baseline that is determined to be adequate by the stakeholders for the organization. These system security controls apply to information systems that reside on yours or someone else's (the cloud) network.

Access control (AC): Organizations must
1. Limit information system access to authorized users, processes acting on behalf of authorized users, or devices (including other information systems).
2. Limit the types of transactions and functions that authorized users are permitted to exercise.
3. Ensure that part of the "onboarding" process includes the new employee reading and acknowledging receipt of the "computer use policy."
4. Develop an automated means to assign, track, authorize, and manage user permissions.

Awareness and training (AT): Organizations must
1. Ensure that managers and users of organizational information systems are made aware of the security risks associated with their activities and of the applicable laws, directives, policies, standards, instructions, regulations, or procedures related to the security of organizational information systems.
2. Ensure that organizational personnel are adequately trained to carry out their assigned information security-related duties and responsibilities. Training must occur at least annually.

Audit and accountability (AU): Organizations must
1. Create, protect, and retain information system audit records to the extent needed to enable the monitoring, analysis,

investigation, and reporting of unlawful, unauthorized, or inappropriate information system activity to support any investigations of those incidents. Additionally, maintaining logs will give you the ability to perform trend analysis and see what major issues and recurring events are taking place.

2. Ensure that the actions of individual information system users can be uniquely traced to those users, so they can be held accountable for their actions. The insider threat still remains the number one vulnerability to an organization.

Compliance and security assessments (CA): Organizations must

1. Periodically assess the security controls in the organizational information systems to determine if the controls are effective in their application; a quarterly assessment of a determined percentage is highly recommended to alleviate an annual network-wide evaluation.

2. Develop and implement plans of action designed to correct deficiencies and reduce or eliminate vulnerabilities in organizational information systems; these should be assessed, tracked, and reviewed by the senior information assurance manager of the organization.

3. Have the senior information assurance manager authorize the operation of organizational information systems and any associated information system connections.

4. Monitor information system security controls on an ongoing basis to ensure the continued effectiveness of the controls and user compliance with the policies.

Configuration management (CM): Organizations must

1. Establish and maintain baseline configurations and inventories of organizational information systems (including hardware, software, firmware, and documentation) throughout the respective system development life cycles.

2. Create or have an automated process as the best approach to enhance the organizational ability to respond to and configure the information systems.

3. Establish and enforce security configuration settings for information technology products employed in organizational information systems.

Contingency planning (CP): Organizations must

1. Establish, maintain, and effectively implement plans for emergency response, backup operations, and postdisaster recovery for organizational information systems to ensure the availability of critical information resources and continuity of operations in emergency situations.
2. Establish emergency occupant plans that coincide with the local area you are in and work with the city, town, or district emergency management system in which your organization is located.

Identification and authentication (IA): Organizations must

1. Identify information system users, processes acting on behalf of users, or devices, and authenticate (or verify) the identities of those users, processes, or devices, as a prerequisite to allowing access to organizational information systems.
2. Develop an automated way of evaluating users and ensuring that they are assigned to the proper groups and that permissions are limited to those applications that they need for their role.
3. Ensure there is an automated way to determine account termination, unused accounts, and passwords that have not been changed over the set number of days as required by organizational policy.

Incident response (IR): Organizations must

1. Establish an operational incident handling capability for organizational information systems that includes adequate preparation, detection, analysis, containment, recovery, and user response activities.
2. Track, document, and report incidents to appropriate organizational officials or authorities.
3. Using an automated system, have sufficient space to maintain incidents for future investigations and track incident reoccurrence for trending and like situations.

Maintenance (MA): Organizations must

1. Perform periodic and timely maintenance on organizational information systems.
2. Provide effective controls on the tools, techniques, mechanisms, and personnel used to conduct information system maintenance.
3. Maintain a record of all maintenance, maintenance personnel, their access, and provide an auditable method for presentation to the configuration control board for validation of events.

Media protection (MP): Organizations must

1. Protect information system media, both paper and digital.
2. Limit access to information on information system media to authorized users by assigning security controls to track directory and file-level assignments.
3. Have a means of tracking transfer of media to and from systems using removable media.
4. Sanitize or destroy information system media before disposal or release for reuse.

Physical and environmental protection (PE): Organizations must

1. Limit physical access to information systems, equipment, and the respective operating environments to authorized individuals.
2. Provide protection for the physical building, parking areas, walkways, and support infrastructure for information systems.
3. Provide primary and backup supporting utilities for information systems.
4. Protect information systems against environmental hazards.
5. Provide remotely monitored and controlled servers in data center environments.
6. Provide appropriate environmental controls in facilities containing information systems.
7. Maintain data center drawings that depict the breakdown of systems, hot and cold row divisions, and provide a functional *emergency power off* (EPO) for situations that demand its capabilities.

Planning (PL): Organizations must

1. Develop, document, periodically update, and implement security plans for organizational information systems that describe the system security controls in place or planned for the information systems, and the rules of behavior for individuals accessing the information systems.
2. Provide, when required, those documents for validation for interconnections that involve other agencies.

Personnel security (PS): Organizations must

1. Ensure that individuals occupying positions of responsibility within organizations (including third-party service providers) are trustworthy and meet established security criteria for those positions.
2. Ensure that organizational information and information systems are protected during and after personnel actions such as terminations and transfers.
3. Employ formal sanctions for personnel failing to comply with organizational security policies and procedures.

Risk assessment (RA): Organizations must

1. Periodically assess the risk to organizational operations (including mission, functions, image, or reputation), organizational assets, and individuals, resulting from the operation of organizational information systems and the associated processing, storage, or transmission of organizational information.
2. Apply due care, review, and update the risk assessment at least annually.

System and services acquisition (SA): Organizations must

1. Allocate sufficient resources to adequately protect organizational information systems.
2. Develop a structure for all requisitions for information systems to be reviewed and signed off by the organization security officer.
3. Employ system development life cycle processes that incorporate information security considerations.
4. Employ software usage and installation restrictions.

5. Ensure that third-party providers employ adequate security measures to protect information, applications, and services outsourced from the organization.

System and communications protection (SC): Organizations must

1. Monitor, control, and protect organizational communications (i.e., information transmitted or received by organizational information systems) at the external boundaries and key internal boundaries of the information systems.
2. Incorporate point-to-point encryption for all "data in motion."
3. Provide encryption for all "data in transit/data at rest" that are moved to a storage facility.
4. Employ architectural designs, software development techniques, and systems engineering principles that promote effective information security within organizational information systems.

System and information integrity (SI): Organizations must

1. Procure or develop an automated process to identify, report, and correct information and information system flaws in a timely manner.
2. Provide protection from malicious code at all locations within an organizational information system.
3. Monitor information system security alerts, prioritize actions and advisories, and take appropriate actions in response and be able to track all responses to the alerts.

Program management (PM): Organizations must

1. Develop, document, and provide all personnel concerned with a security program plan.
2. Assign a senior information security officer that has the overall development, responsibility, and design of the enterprise infrastructure.
3. Maintain an inventory of all enterprise information security resources.
4. Develop a plan of action and milestones (POA&M) process that tracks the vulnerabilities, system, corrective actions, responsible personnel, and costs.

5. Maintain an updated information system inventory that shows each system, the electrical resources needed for each system, the switch port numbers, and the system administrators assigned to each information system.
6. Track and maintain information security measures of performance, bandwidth usage, and application ports.
7. Develop an enterprise architecture plan that identifies current state and planned growth.
8. Document the critical infrastructure plan.
9. Develop, document, and maintain a risk management strategy.
10. Have in place a security authorization process that is repeatable throughout the enterprise architecture.
11. Document the business process definition as assigned to each enclave, information system group, or information system.

Although developing a system security categorization is a very in-depth task, it is the foundation on which security is built and maintained. With security as your foundation, you should begin to see how each and every process that follows is a by-product of a secure enterprise infrastructure.

Each chapter in this book speaks to building that foundation and building the security that is required to protect the infrastructure. As we move forward and see that industrial espionage, insider threats, and malicious code pose the biggest threats to maintaining a posture, I believe that it is better to have something in place when you need it vs. needing it and not having it. Take control and develop or redevelop your enterprise to reach the goals of true security over just wishing you had done so when it is too late!

5

BUSINESS IMPACT ANALYSIS

Business impact analysis (BIA) is the one document that starts the process and actually feeds the entire document set for compliance requirements; your organization's future resides with a complete analysis. It should be regarded as the most important process when considering the system development life cycle (SDLC) and advancing your network infrastructure.

Note: Without documentation you cannot validate that you do something, or at least say you have procedures that are standardized. The normal processes of effective IT management are

- **Policy:** Documented proof that you have a requirement.
- **Procedures:** You have a managed process for performing the steps.
- **Implementation:** You are performing the technical aspects of the requirements.
- **Tested:** Your policy and procedures are working.
- **Integration/maintenance:** You review your policy and procedures at the managerial, operational, and technical levels for change and update the policy and procedures.

The hierarchy of business and IT management was part of the National Institute of Standards and Technology (NIST) Special Publication (SP) 800-26, which is no longer current but has strategic and methodical procedures that incorporate the managerial, operational, and technical aspects of managing an IT portfolio.

The three steps that follow depict the 30,000-foot level of involvement in accomplishing the BIA; when you break each of these down you will find that the total actual steps far exceed the three identified on the next page. These steps help you get moving and understand what needs to be accomplished. We will discover more of this as we move forward through this and the other chapters. I will attempt to explain this further in the examples provided; use these steps as your guide to a beginning:

1. *Determine mission/business processes and recovery criticality.* Mission/business processes supported by the system (s) are identified and the impact of a system disruption to those processes is determined along with outage impacts and estimated downtime. The downtime should reflect the maximum time that an organization can tolerate while still maintaining the mission.
2. *Identify resource requirements.* Realistic recovery efforts require a thorough evaluation of the resources required to resume mission/business processes and related interdependencies as quickly as possible. Examples of resources that should be identified include facilities, personnel, equipment, software, data files, system components, and vital records.
3. *Identify recovery priorities for system resources.* Based upon the results from the previous activities, system resources can be linked more clearly to critical mission/business processes and functions. Priority levels can be established for sequencing recovery activities and resources.

Once the BIA report is delivered, the BIA is not complete; it should be evaluated during the risk assessment process and incorporated into, and tested as part of, the business continuity plan (BCP). The BIA should be reviewed by the board and senior management periodically and updated to reflect significant changes in business operations, audit recommendations, and lessons learned during the testing process—many other aspects of the BIA include a vigorous involvement of management at all levels and include

1. Business continuity plan development
   a. Staff training
   b. Business continuity plan validation
       i. Drills
       ii. Exercises
2. Configuration management plan (updating or development)
3. Capital planning and investment control (CPIC)
4. Disaster recovery plan updating, developing, and testing
5. Program effectiveness evaluation and monitoring

What Is the Business Impact Analysis?

The business impact analysis (BIA) is the core of a business, and as shown previously, the BIA will feed each and every one of the areas covered for a good start—many other aspects of your infrastructure are yet to be refined or developed.

A BIA is the foundation of a business, business functioning, and business ability to recover; it is the key to a successful disaster recovery (DR) strategy and plan. A BIA is used to identify the processes, systems, and functions that are critical to the survival of your company. The BIA is used to not only identify what your core processing requirements are, but also identify what priority each system or application is in the recovery process. Understanding these elements allows you to allocate resources wisely to ensure operations even with unexpected events disrupting normal business operations.

A business impact analysis is an investigative process that aims to expose the business impacts that would result when a critical process exceeds its maximum allowable outage.

To start, you need to understand the business operations of the company, in detail, not just that you have the administrative section, human relations department, finance department, marketing, and whatever else. An effective BIA uses a step-by-step approach that will put you on your way to conducting a successful business impact analysis. Before we get into the meat and potatoes of this section, let's explore the definition of what a business impact analysis really is:

Taken from NIST, BIA is a crucial component of an organization's business continuity plan; it includes an *exploratory component* to reveal any vulnerabilities and a *planning component* to develop strategies for minimizing risk. The result of analysis is a business impact analysis report, which describes the potential risks specific to the organization studied. One of the basic assumptions behind BIA is that every component of the organization is reliant upon the continued functioning of every other component, but that some are more crucial than others and require a greater allocation of funds in the wake of a disaster. For example, a business may be able to continue more or less normally if the cafeteria has to close, but would come to a complete halt if the information system crashes.

As part of a disaster recovery plan, BIA is likely to identify costs linked to failures, such as loss of cash flow, replacement of equipment, salaries paid to catch up with a backlog of work, loss of profits, and so on. A BIA report quantifies the importance of business components and suggests appropriate fund allocation for measures to protect them. The possibilities of failures are likely to be assessed in terms of their impacts on safety, finances, marketing, legal compliance, and quality assurance. Where possible, impact is expressed monetarily for purposes of comparison. For example, a business may spend three times as much on marketing in the wake of a disaster to rebuild customer confidence.

Objectives of the Business Impact Analysis

The core business of your organization is to produce a product and make a profit from the sales and provide your dedicated staff with an income to support their families, both of which are mission critical; one does not exist without the other. Therefore, the most significant impact of a disaster upon the organization would be disruption of production and research programs that make the product better and cheaper. Disruption of the organization and research programs for a period of time greater than one week would be very damaging to the organization's mission.

The purpose of a business impact analysis is to identify and prioritize mission-critical functions and processes that make up the organization and its ability to produce the product. The inability to perform these functions would significantly impact the company's core mission.

The BIA is a tool to identify what processes need to be continued, in what priority, any dependencies, and the supporting resources. In other words, it is foundation for any recovery or disruption plan development. The development of a working business impact analysis is more than determining the recovery time objective (RTO) or the recovery point objective (RPO); these are outcomes of a full and complete BIA and result in a model that determines what is acceptable for the mission. An additional product of the BIA is the more defined maximum tolerable downtime (MTD) of each application and supporting servers. All three—RTO, RPO, and MTD—are feeds into the disaster recovery plan.

Developing the Project Plan

Three steps are typically involved in accomplishing the BIA:

1. *Determine mission/business functions and recovery criticality.* Mission/business functions supported by the system are identified, and the impact of a system disruption to those functions is determined along with outage impacts and estimated downtime. The downtime should reflect the maximum time that an organization can tolerate while still maintaining the mission.
2. *Identify resource requirements.* Realistic recovery efforts require a thorough evaluation of the resources required to resume mission/business functions and related interdependencies as quickly as possible. Examples of resources that should be identified include facilities, personnel, equipment, software, data files, system components, and vital records.
3. *Identify recovery priorities for system resources.* Based upon the results from the previous activities, system resources can be linked more clearly to critical mission/business processes and functions. Priority levels can be established for sequencing recovery activities and resources.

Recovery priorities are based on the business model and how much and how long the data can be "stale" or lost. Recovery priorities use simple terms such as recovery point objective (RPO) and recovery time objective (RTO). RPO is the maximum desired time period prior to a failure or disaster during which changes to data may be lost as a consequence of recovery. Data changes preceding the failure or disaster by at least this time period are preserved by recovery. Zero is a valid value and is equivalent to a zero data loss requirement. RTO is the duration of time and a service level within which a business process must be restored after a disaster in order to avoid unacceptable consequences associated with a break in business continuity. Each of these, as stated, are based on the business model and permissible staleness of the data and can be based on what your customers believe is relevant; e.g., the recovery point objective of a payroll system (depending on your payroll cycle) may be as little as hours, and the recovery time objectives may be based on minutes, not hours. In this case you would have redundant systems with failover, but it is still important to include this within the BIA as the recovery priority. Maximum tolerable downtime (MTD) represents the total amount of time leaders/managers are willing to accept for a mission/business process outage or disruption and includes all impact considerations.

BIA Process Steps

To keep it simple (it is never simple), I use the guide of a five-phase project development. Within each of the following phases, I identify the key points to the phase and any comments that may enlighten you to understand what the requirements are for the phase or step. Do not kid yourself; a typical business impact analysis should take five personnel (familiar with each other) approximately four months for a company of medium growth ($25 million per year). The personnel needed for completion are

- **Team leader (TL):** The TL does not do any discovery; the position is a leadership position and a manager's position. You must be on site to interact with the client and let it know what is needed and what progress has been made. The TL should have technical and managerial experience.
- **Senior technical person:** The senior technical person (regardless of title) should know all systems, mainframe, AIX (P Series), single-system servers, and local/wide area network (LAN/WAN) technologies, and be familiar with small to medium business (SMB) applications. This person should be certified to the maximum and have the experience to back up the certifications.
- **Mid-term technical person:** At least two certified and well-positioned personnel that understand but have not had all the experience a senior person would (obviously). Someone that is at the Microsoft Certified System Engineer (MCSE)/Cisco Certified Network Professional (CCNP)/system administration level of their career. Education is always good, but most are working on their degrees or just finished—the learner! Someone that you can rely on to perform the tasks at hand and trust the completion is at or above standard.

- **Technical writer (TW):** Worth their weight in gold. Nothing can replace a good TW; the more years of experience, the better, and a person's pay scale might be a limiting factor, but do your best. They should know and understand all aspects and all terminology of the field; if not, go somewhere else. They should also be able to take that terminology and produce layperson term documents at the executive level. They should know that an executive summary is no more than two pages—preferably one. My experience has introduced me to one great TW; they are few and far between.

Now that your team is ready, let's take a look at the project plan; understand your company might have templates that look nothing like this. This is just an example—not a gospel. Besides, I am not writing about project plans!

Once the project team is formed, the activities on project planning and execution can begin. There are five stages of project progression within the project discovery phase that will move you into the next step of the project; this may be your final step, but in the overall project you are just a piece of the puzzle. The five stages are as follows:

1. Initiation and development
2. Discovery and collection
3. Application and data criticality
4. Data analysis
5. Final reports/presentations

Initiation and development: An idea for a project will be carefully examined to determine whether or not it benefits the organization. During this phase, a decision-making team will identify if the project can realistically be completed in the time frame allocated; a lot depends on the size of the organization and the personnel involved (contractor/employee). The development of a complete plan will take a few tries unless you have templates from years of experience—I have yet to see one plan include all the variables. During this phase, a team should prioritize the project, calculate a budget and schedule, and determine what resources are needed.

Discovery and collection: A project plan and project scope should always be put in writing, outlining the work to be performed. To do a complete discovery you will need stakeholder involvement, and it should be stressed to them that they need to define specific personnel that are your "go to persons" for any access to controlled areas, issues with obtaining data, or just overall project support. Discovery takes the longest time and should—you are trying to find everything there is about every major application, every general support system, and maybe even a minor application.

I have seen batch jobs considered a major application, and the organization received thousands of dollars a year for support of that application. The application contained about five lines of code to transfer data from one database to another. Now that is cost-effective computing!

Application and data criticality: Looking at the organization's applications and determining the criticality takes stakeholder input. When you look at these applications and ask the correct questions, don't forget to ask: When was the last time they did without the application during a test?

Project performance and control: Project managers will compare project status and progress to the actual plan, as resources perform the scheduled work. During this phase, project managers may need to adjust schedules or do what is necessary to keep the project on track. One major part of the performance and control phase is to maintain control of the cost of the project and the milestones. Performance can be based off of dollars and time, but it should not be a determining factor. Using dollars to measure efficiency can be detrimental to the overall outcome of your performance measures.

Instead, use your established milestones over the conduct of the project with established dollar values for the time period. Within the project management area it is called the earned value management system (EVMS). EVMS was developed by the U.S. Army, and since then there have been a few different models; they all boil down to milestones (tasks) and dollars of time. Many models are available to determine your budget and costs, so choose the style that best suits you and your project requirements. Most planners use a project management control system (PMCS) that is engraved within the company, so be familiar with the requirements and the contract.

Managing the team is one of the most critical aspects of project management. This involves not only managing internal staff, but also managing any customer personnel and subcontractors assigned to the project team.

Key facets of effective project management include those responsibilities that include the people aspect of leadership:

- Delegating responsibility for work assignments and witnessing the commitment of each team member
- Building cooperative working relationships and ensuring effective communications among all members of the project team
- Monitoring team morale and taking action to correct problem areas
- Providing effective performance review and appraisal to motivate staff and facilitate career development

The subprocesses are

1. **Set up standards and procedures for team performance:** As a key element in ensuring a quality project, make sure that team members have been involved in the development of common standards and procedures for anything that impacts the general conduct of the team.

2. **Assign responsibilities:** Meet with the individuals responsible for each milestone and review objectives and assign responsibility to the right leader. Make sure there is a mutual understanding and commitment to the project's milestones and expectations of each person and that each person is to produce, the quality requirements for each milestone, the standards and procedures to be followed, and the cost estimates and schedule that each person is being asked to commit, as a team.

3. **Meet with team:** Conduct weekly or biweekly meetings with team leaders to review issues, share experiences, and resolve problems and concerns. Make sure that team leaders hold similar meetings with their team members,

and that identified issues are recorded, communicated, and followed through to closure.

4. **Communicate project information:** On a small project, effective communication may require nothing more than routine, informal interaction among the team. On a project with multiple subprojects or a distributed project team, a more formal communications process needs to define the tasks, track the progress, and help define the timelines. Outlook with an integrated portal server works great when you integrate a project server into the mix—explore your options and cost realizations for the size of the project.

5. **Recognize success:** Praise in public and punish in private. There is nothing more damaging to a project than to have a manager filling a leadership position without the knowledge and experience of a leader and flying off on a simple matter and making it a mountain. Awards can be used for short-term recognition, but level the reward to the task and project savings.

6. **Monitor team morale:** A real leader knows his or her people and knows when performance falls, there is an issue. Something as little as a misunderstanding can curtail a project and cut profits and milestones. Pizza lunch or a nice dinner can go miles on a project; once again, weigh the rewards to the project and task.

7. **Conduct team performance reviews:** This is a task that should be performed at each level; an initial review and then every six months tells the employee that you care about them and that you have these expectations of them. There is nothing worse than having a leader not speak to teams. Every team leader should evaluate his or her people, and the project manager/deputy manager performs the team leader's evaluation.

Project close: In the weeks nearing the closure of a project the project manager should be in conversation with the client multiple times in each day. Ensure as you complete tasks you give an informal daily brief and weekly wrap-up to all stakeholders. Ensure that you have some form of formal sign-off for each of the milestones. After project tasks are completed and the client has approved the outcome, an evaluation is necessary to highlight project success or learn from project history. Outside the client site conduct a formal after action review (AAR) with the team within five days of project closure.

Performing the BIA

We have discovered that the business impact analysis (BIA) is the foundation for all business continuity planning programs. It identifies the financial and operational influences that may result from a disruption of business operations. NIST SP 800-60, volume II, defines the disruptions that can take place and include, for example:

- Short-term, due to a power interruption or information systems hardware issue.
- Long-term, due to a fire or natural disaster. Regardless of the disruption's source, business operations are compromised.

Understanding how an outage could affect your business is vital to making the right decisions to protect your company's assets and manage risk. A BIA should be conducted whether you are preparing a plan for your manufacturing operations or developing plans for all of your organization's facilities. Key factors are defined in NIST SP 800-60, volume II, and can be applied across any infrastructure.

Conducting a BIA helps define the impacts or concerns of losing individual business operations and analyzes the effects of these impacts over defined time frames. Impacts usually fall into two major categories: financial and operational. Financial impacts, such as lost sales and contract penalties, are quickly reflected in the bottom line. Operational impacts, such as loss of market share or loss of investor confidence, often occur more slowly and with more devastating results. By understanding the potential impacts, senior management can make informed decisions about business continuity and risk management strategies.

More specifically, a BIA provides the following information for the business continuity planner:

- Financial impacts by business operation, location, and for the organization as a whole

- Operations impacts by business operation, location, and for the organization as a whole
- Extraordinary expenses needed to continue operations after a business interruption
- Organization's current state of preparedness
- Technological requirements for resumption and recovery
- Special resources
- Process support for resumption and recovery operations

There are generally four globular steps included in the BIA process (you will do this for every system):

1. Gathering information
2. Performing a vulnerability assessment
3. Analyzing the information
4. Documenting the results and presenting the recommendations

Gathering Information

The first step of the BIA is to identify which departments and business processes are critical to the recovery of the financial institution. The business continuity planning committee or coordinator should review organizational charts, observe daily workflow, and interview department managers and employees to identify critical functions and significant interrelationships on an enterprise-wide basis. Information can also be gathered using surveys, questionnaires, and team meetings.

As information is gathered and critical operations are identified, business operations and related interdependencies should be reviewed to establish processing priorities between departments and alternate operating procedures that can be utilized during recovery.

Performing a Vulnerability Assessment

A vulnerability assessment is similar to a risk assessment; however, it focuses solely on providing information that will be used in the business continuity planning process. The goal of the vulnerability assessment is to determine the potential impact of disruptive events on the financial institution's business processes. Financial industry participants should consider the impact of a major disruption since they play a critical role in the financial system. As part of the vulnerability assessment, a loss impact analysis should be conducted that defines loss criteria as either quantitative (financial) or qualitative (operational). For example, quantitative losses may consist of declining revenues, increasing capital expenditures, or personal liability issues. Conversely, qualitative losses may consist of declining market share or loss of public confidence. While performing a vulnerability assessment, you should identify critical support areas and related interdependencies, which are defined as a department or process that must be properly functioning to sustain operations, to determine the overall impact of a disruptive event. In addition, required personnel, resources, and services used to maintain these support areas must also be identified. Critical support areas and interdependencies should include the following, at a minimum:

- Communications media
- IT departments
- Transportation and delivery services
- Shared physical facilities, equipment, hardware, and software
- Third-party vendors
- Back-office operations, including accounting, payroll, transaction processing, customer service, and purchasing

The steps needed to perform a vulnerability assessment include the following:

1. List applicable threats (see NIST SP 800-30 for defining threats) that may occur internally and externally.
2. Estimate the likelihood that each threat might occur.
3. Assess the potential impact of the threat on employees and customers, property, and business operations.
4. Assess the internal and external resources available to deal with the identified threats.

Analyzing the Information

During the analysis phase of the BIA, results of the vulnerability assessment should be analyzed and interpreted to determine the overall impact of various threats on the financial institution. This analysis process should include an estimation of maximum allowable downtime (MAD) that can be tolerated by the financial institution as a result of a disruptive event. MAD estimates that may be used include the following:

- Nonessential—30 days
- Normal—7 days
- Important—72 hours
- Urgent—24 hours
- Critical—minutes to hours

Each business function and process should be placed in one of these categories so that management can determine applicable solutions to ensure timely recovery of operations. Management should then determine which business functions represent the highest priority for recovery and establish recovery objectives for these critical operations. The business continuity planning committee or coordinator should discuss the impact of all possible disruptive events, instead of focusing on specific events that may never occur. For example, the impact of a disruptive event could result in equipment failure, destruction of facilities, data corruption, and the lack of available personnel, supplies, vendors, or service providers. Once the impact of a disruption is determined, management should estimate MADs.

After completing the data analysis, the results should be reviewed by knowledgeable employees to ensure that the findings are representative of the true risks and ultimate impact faced by the financial institution. If notable gaps are identified, they should be recognized and incorporated into the overall analysis.

Documenting the Results and Presenting the Recommendations

The final step of the BIA involves documenting all of the processes, procedures, analyses, and results. Once the BIA is complete, a report should be presented to the board and senior management identifying critical departments and processes, significant interdependencies, a summary of the vulnerability assessment, and recommended recovery priorities generated from the analysis.

6

RISK

Risk Management

Managing information system-related security risk is a complex, multifaceted undertaking that requires the involvement of the entire organization—from senior leaders providing the strategic vision and top-level goals and objectives for the organization, to mid-level leaders planning and managing projects, to individuals on the front lines developing, implementing, and operating the systems supporting the organization's core missions and business processes. Risk management can be viewed as a holistic activity that is fully integrated into every aspect of the organization. Figure 6.1 illustrates a three-tiered approach to risk management that addresses risk-related concerns at

1. The organization level
2. The mission and business process level
3. The information system level

The risk process can be detailed within four specific steps:

1. Framing risk within the organization
2. How the organization evaluates or assesses risk
3. How the organization responds or reacts to the risk mitigation process
4. How the organization monitors current risk, mitigates risk, and reviews the development of new risk

In a more detailed approach, the following four sections identify each of the above steps and further attempt to define the process and procedures for risk acceptance and mitigation.

Framework

An organization must first review and develop a risk framework in which it looks at the threat motivators and content and how

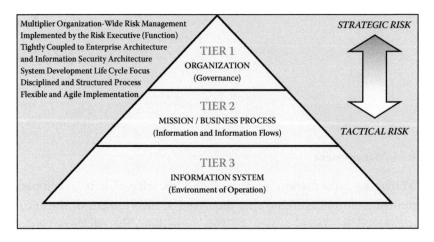

Figure 6.1 NIST three-tiered risk approach.

a risk-based decision (RBD) is made in the mitigation process. The purpose of risk framing is to produce a risk management strategy that addresses how organizations intend to assess risk, respond to risk, and monitor risk—making explicit and transparent the risk perceptions that organizations routinely use in making both investment and operational decisions. As one of the prodigies of security, the risk frame establishes a foundation for managing risk, as security builds the structure to support the risk-based decisions, and binds the RBD of an organization to its practices and procedures.

Establishing a realistic and credible risk frame requires that organizations identify the following:

1. Risk assumptions (e.g., assumptions about threats, vulnerabilities, consequences/impact, and likelihood of occurrence that affect how risk is assessed, responded to, and monitored).
2. Risk constraints (e.g., constraints on the risk assessment, risk response, and risk monitoring alternatives under consideration).
3. Risk tolerance (e.g., levels of risk, types of risk, and degree of risk uncertainty that are acceptable).
4. Priorities and trade-offs (e.g., relative importance of missions/business functions, trade-offs among different types of risk that organizations face, time frames in which organizations must address risk, and any factors of uncertainty that organizations consider in risk responses). The risk framing

component and the associated risk management strategy also include any strategic-level decisions on how risk to organizational operations and assets, individuals, other organizations, and the nation is to be managed by senior leaders/executives.

Assessment or Evaluation

To further manage risk, an organization must address how it assesses or evaluates risk within the context of the organizational risk frame. The purpose of the risk assessment component is to identify the following:

1. Threats to organizations (i.e., operations, assets, or individuals) or threats directed through organizations against other organizations or the nation
2. Vulnerabilities, internal and external, to organizations
3. The harm (i.e., consequences/impact) to organizations that may occur given the potential for threats exploiting vulnerabilities
4. The likelihood that harm will occur

The end result is a determination of risk (i.e., considering the risk tolerance level in the degree of harm and the likelihood and frequency of the event occurring or reoccurring). To support the risk assessment component, organizations identify the following:

1. The tools, techniques, and methodologies that are used to assess risk
2. The assumptions related to risk assessments
3. The constraints that may affect risk assessments
4. Roles and responsibilities
5. How risk assessment information is collected, processed, and communicated throughout organizations
6. How risk assessments are conducted within organizations
7. The frequency of risk assessments
8. How threat information is obtained (i.e., sources and methods)

Mitigation and Response

Risk mitigation and response addresses how organizations *respond or mitigate* risk once that risk is determined based on the results of risk assessments. The purpose of the risk response and mitigation phase is to provide a dependable, organization-wide response to risk in accordance with the organizational risk frame by

1. Developing alternative courses of action for responding to risk
2. Evaluating the alternative courses of action
3. Determining appropriate courses of action consistent with organizational risk tolerance
4. Implementing risk responses based on selected courses of action stemming from the baseline security requirements, policies, and procedures

To support the risk response phase, organizations describe the types of risk responses that can be implemented (i.e., accepting, avoiding, mitigating, sharing, or transferring risk). Transferring risk refers to an organization obtaining an insurance policy from an insurance company that specializes in information technology risk (i.e., IT risk managers). The U.S. government does not transfer risk, but instead focuses on the system (software or hardware) development life cycle (SDLC) to bring the probability of risk to an acceptable factor. Organizations also identify the tools, techniques, and methodologies used to develop courses of action for responding to risk, how courses of action are evaluated, and how risk responses are communicated across organizations and, as appropriate, to external entities (e.g., external service providers, supply chain partners).

Monitoring

Risk monitoring addresses how organizations monitor risk over time and the type of data collected. An important part of risk monitoring is once the data are collected, what you do with those data. Managers need to look for trends, anomalies, and instances of abnormal behavior within the infrastructure, but to do this you need a baseline. The baseline can be obtained over an initial period, and then over time and maturity your monitoring grows and your organization becomes proactive vs. reactive. The purpose of the risk monitoring component is to

1. Verify that needed risk response measures are implemented and information security requirements derived from/traceable to organizational missions/business functions, federal legislation, directives, regulations, policies, standards, and guidelines are satisfied

2. Determine the ongoing effectiveness of risk response measures postimplementation
3. Identify risk-impacting changes to organizational information systems and the environments in which the systems operate

To support risk monitoring, organizations describe how compliance is verified and how the ongoing effectiveness of risk responses is determined (e.g., the types of tools, techniques, and methodologies used to determine the sufficiency/correctness of risk responses and if risk mitigation measures are implemented correctly, operating as intended, and producing the desired effect with regard to reducing risk). In addition, organizations describe how changes that may impact the ongoing effectiveness of risk responses are monitored. Risk monitoring has a by-product stage of leveraging your return on investment (ROI) for the tools and procedures used in this phase by determining what works best and what results provide the best return. The U.S. government software list has recommended vendors of software items that have provided proven results.

Risk Assessment

The risk assessment is the second step in the business continuity planning (BCP) process. It should include the following:

- Evaluating the BIA assumptions using various threat scenarios
- Analyzing threats based upon the impact to the institution, its customers, and the financial market it serves
- Prioritizing potential business disruptions based upon their severity, which is determined by their impact on operations and the probability of occurrence
- Performing a gap analysis that compares the existing BCP to the policies and procedures that should be implemented based on prioritized disruptions identified and their resulting impact on the institution

The risk assessment step is critical and has significant bearing on whether business continuity planning efforts will be successful. During the risk assessment step, business processes and the BIA assumptions are evaluated using various threat scenarios. This will result in a range of outcomes that may require changes to the BCP.

Financial institutions should develop realistic threat scenarios that may potentially disrupt business processes and their ability to meet clients' expectations (internal, business partners, or customers). Threats can take many forms, including malicious activity, natural and technical disasters, and pandemic incidents. Where possible, institutions should analyze a threat by using nonspecific, all-risk planning that focuses on the impact of the threat instead of the nature of the threat. For example, the effects of certain threat scenarios can include business disruptions that affect only specific personnel, work areas, systems, facilities (i.e., buildings), or geographic areas. Additionally, the magnitude of the business disruption should consider a wide variety of threat scenarios based upon practical experiences and potential circumstances and events. If the threat scenarios are not comprehensive, the resulting BCP may be too basic and omit reasonable steps that are needed for a timely recovery after a disruption.

Threat scenarios should consider the severity of the disaster, which is based upon the impact and probability of business disruptions resulting from identified threats. Threats may range from those with a high probability of occurrence and low impact to the institution, such as brief power interruptions, to those with a low probability of occurrence and high impact to the institution, such as hurricanes or terrorist attacks. The most difficult threats to address are those that have a high impact on the institution but a low probability of occurrence. However, through the use of nonspecific, all-risk planning, the BCP may be more flexible and adaptable to all types of disruptions.

When assessing the probability of a disruption, financial institutions and technology service providers should consider the geographic location of all facilities, their susceptibility to threats (e.g., location in a floodplain), and the proximity to critical infrastructures (e.g., power sources, nuclear power plants, airports, major highways, railroads). Worst-case scenarios, such as destruction of the facilities and loss of life, should be considered. As part of this process, external factors should also be closely monitored to determine the probability of occurrence. External factors can be monitored through constant communication with community and government officials and regulatory authorities. For example, institutions should monitor alerts issued by such organizations as the Department of Homeland Security and the World Health Organization, which provide information regarding terrorist activity and environmental risks, respectively.

After analyzing the impact, probability, and resulting severity of identified threats, the institution can prioritize business processes and estimate how they could be disrupted under various threat scenarios. The resulting probability of occurrence may be based on a rating system of high, medium, and low.

At this point in the business continuity planning process, the organization should perform a gap analysis. In this context, a gap analysis is a methodical comparison of what types of policies and procedures the institution (or business line) should implement to recover, resume, and maintain normal business operations vs. what the existing BCP provides. The difference between the two highlights additional risk exposure that management should address when developing the BCP.

7
SECURE CONFIGURATION MANAGEMENT

Secure configuration management (SCM) is the root of your security program. Using SCM will demonstrate how everything else that goes on within an organization is a by-product of security. The SCM program manages security features and assurances through control of changes made to the hardware, software, firmware, documentation, test, and test documentation throughout the life cycle of an information system.

SCM is an ongoing process of

1. Planning for the system and designing a life cycle using industry standards
2. Identifying assets or configuration items (CIs)
3. Documenting the steps taken and projected steps of the process
4. Managing changes to all aspects of the planning, design, implementation, change, and monitoring phases
5. Monitoring your project through a business security approach

Managing changes to deliverables, information systems are designed and operate in many configurations and can be interconnected in many different arrangements to meet a variety of business, mission, and information security requirements. How these information system components are networked, configured, and managed is critical in providing adequate information security and supporting an organization's risk management process. Hopefully by now you can see that by using the risk management framework and security configuration, your infrastructure can be based on the security model.

In reading this chapter, I hope you develop a good understanding of what to do to develop and maintain a security configuration management process and how to develop a secure configuration management plan. Both terms are used interchangeably; it is the act of performing configuration management using and keeping security as your basis of decision making and portfolio management.

An information system is typically in a constant state of change in response to new, enhanced, corrected, or updated hardware and software capabilities, patches for correcting software flaws and other errors to existing components, new security threats, changing business functions, etc. Implementing information system changes almost always results in some adjustment to the system configuration. To ensure that the required adjustments to the system configuration do not adversely affect the security of the information system or the organization from operation of the information system, a well-defined configuration management process that integrates information security is needed.

Organizations apply security configuration management for establishing baselines and for tracking, controlling, and managing many aspects of business development and operation (e.g., products, services, manufacturing, business processes, and information technology). Organizations with a robust and effective SCM process need to consider information security implications with respect to the development and operation of information systems, including hardware, software, applications, and documentation. Effective SCM of information systems requires the integration of the management of secure configurations into the organizational SCM process or processes. For this reason, this chapter assumes that information security is an integral part of an organization's overall SCM process; however, the focus of this chapter is on implementation of the information system security aspects of SCM, and as such the term *security-focused configuration management* (SCM) is used to emphasize the concentration on information security. Though both IT business application functions and security-focused practices are expected to be integrated as a single process, SCM in this context is defined as the management and control of configurations for information systems to enable security and facilitate the management of information security risk within the business processes and complement the business model by protecting those systems that build the infrastructure.

Phases of Security-Focused Configuration Management

Security configuration management of information systems involves a disciplined set of activities that can be organized into five major phases:

1. Planning: Each change, procedure, and policy should be based on a business plan that coexists with the business model.
2. Identifying and design: Doing so to each system and documenting it throughout the life cycle.
3. Implementing configurations: Those that have been programmed through each phase of the policies, procedures, testing, implementation, and continuous monitoring phases.
4. Controlling configuration changes: By implementation of a technical review or configuration control board that authorized and programs change.
5. Continuous monitoring: So you know what is present, what is happening, and what needs to be accomplished to maintain a secure environment.

It is through these phases that SCM supports security for an information system and its components, but also supports the management of organizational risk (Figure 7.1).

SCM relies upon performance, functional, and physical attributes of IT platforms and products and the environments that they are subjected to in order to determine the appropriate security features and assurances that are used to measure a system configuration state. No system should be placed into any environment, internal or external to the corporate infrastructure, without being properly planned and configured.

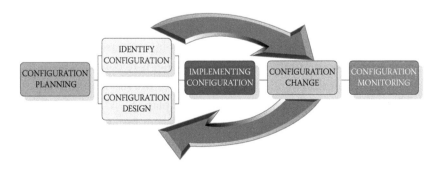

Figure 7.1 Phases of security-focused configuration management.

SCM is established as part of the enterprise security management (ESM) process. The roles and responsibilities for the SCM program management office (PMO) within the organization should be defined, such that the systems meet the stakeholders' needs, the business needs, and industry best practices. The entire organization has a primary responsibility for the safe, secure, and consistent operation of an IT system. Throughout the SCM program, many operational requirements have been directed and defined to automate enterprise vulnerability and configuration management assessment and reporting activities. Determining where you stand and where you need to be can be best determined through the use of a gap analysis. This can be performed by using trusted contractors or internally with qualified personnel under direct management of the CIO and not the manager, so as not to cause an implied or actual conflict of interest.

Using Figure 7.2, the SCM process is overarching of all areas of IT management within an organization. A complete and documented configuration management plan as defined through the National Institute of Standards and Technology lays out a repeatable process to develop, implement, and monitor your program without undue costs to the budget and will ensure you comply with all regulatory requirements.

The continuous monitoring aspects of your enterprise are full aggregation of the assets and maintaining transparency to the stakeholders so they can provide the decision support aspects of infrastructure improvements and growth. Portfolio management as you see ranges across a few areas, meaning that the portfolio dictates, responds, and fulfills a full strategy of responsibilities and is one of the main gap points in communications with management and stakeholders.

The risk management segment also stretches across the enterprise and is the responsibility of the entire organization. The insider threat remains the biggest risk even though malicious hacking has risen some 460% over the past few years. One of the biggest reasons for a sound and exercised configuration management plan is to control your assets and improve on the overall delivery aspects of the service and security.

The security configuration management plan (SCMP) is developed to define, document, control, implement, account for, and audit changes to the various components or configuration items (CIs) of the enterprise. The CMP is the first step in the security configuration management process and is required to provide a repeatable process that produces

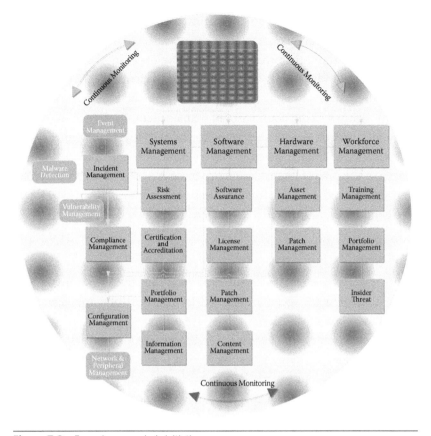

Figure 7.2 Example gap analysis initiative.

like results in each step of SCM. Without a repeatable, documented process, an organization will start to develop multiple methods of doing SCM, and therefore create vulnerabilities that do not need to exist.

Security Configuration Management Plan

The SCMP provides information on the requirements and procedures necessary for SCM activities, and establishes the methodology for configuration identification and control of releases and changes to CIs. It also describes the process for maintaining status accounting and verifying the completeness and correctness of configuration items throughout the system life cycle. Once the SCMP is complete, it will enhance the impact of the business impact analysis and reduce the risks for an organization through a defined boundary of CIs, management of the CIs, and structure for reporting and tracking in the portfolio of each CI.

It is important that the SCMP is developed in the early project development and planning stages to support the items and document the procedures needed to replicate the development and ensure the items are placed within specific boundaries of management. In developing a security configuration management process you need to provide a brief system overview describing the system, its environment, and the development stages of the project and ensure management understands its placement and operational goals for the business architecture. When developing the boundaries, as in the BIA, you need to include the following:

- Responsible division.
- System name or title.
- System code (this is an internal code that tracks funding and management, usually assigned by the portfolio manager or procurement division).
- System category, as determined during the initial design phase:
  - Major application: Performs clearly defined functions for which there are a readily identifiable security consideration and need.
  - Minor application: The application rests within a GSS and receives its security configuration from the GSS.
  - General support system: Provides general information system or network support for a variety of users and applications.
- Operational status:
  - Operational
  - Under development
  - Undergoing a major modification
- System environment or special conditions: This could include any special precautions or configuration that needs special attention or specific procedures that are outside the normal administrative process.

Provide a list of the points of organizational contact (POCs) who may be needed by the document user for informational and troubleshooting purposes. Include type of contact, contact name, department, telephone number, and email address (if applicable). Points of contact may include, but are not limited to, helpdesk POC, development/ maintenance POC, and operations POC.

A list of the POCs who may be needed for informational or troubleshooting purposes as identified below.

CONTACT	CONTACT INFORMATION
[Name]	[Type of contact or specialty]
[Title]	Phone: [XXX-XXX-XXXX]
[Department]	Email: XXX@yourcompany.net
[Name]	[Type of contact or specialty]
[Title]	Phone: [XXX-XXX-XXXX]
[Department]	Email: XXX@yourcompany.net
[Name]	[Type of contact or specialty]
[Title]	Phone: [XXX-XXX-XXXX]
[Department]	Email: XXX@yourcompany.net

Coordination

Organizations that require coordination between the project and its specific support function (installation coordination, security, etc.) are identified below along with a schedule for coordination activities.

ORGANIZATION UNIT	SUPPORT FUNCTION	SCHEDULE
HR	Technically qualified personnel	Monthly
Financial systems	Budget approval	Quarterly
Business development	Portfolio management	Monthly to quarterly
IT	Infrastructure development	Monthly (CCB/TRB)

Configuration Control

Configuration control is the systematic evaluation, coordination, approval or disapproval, and implementation of all proposed changes in the configuration of a configuration item after formal establishment of its baseline. Procedures must be established to ensure that changes are accomplished in an organized manner with traceability and accountability so that project SCM and portfolio management requirements are properly implemented. Requested changes to software, hardware, data, networks, or documentation are formally reviewed and approved in order to allow evaluation of the effect of the change on security, performance, interfaces, acceptability, completeness, and documentation.

Configuration control discusses the systematic proposal, justification, evaluation, coordination, approval or disapproval of proposed changes, and the implementation of all approved changes to a system, regardless of its security category (low, moderate, or high). In performing the tasks as defined, you must look at how and what your change control board (CCB) or technical review board (TRB) operates and what requirements it needs to meet to satisfy the stakeholders and security requirements, which include meeting the business model as its objective.

Change Control Board (CCB) or Technical Review Board (TRB)

The change control board (CCB) or technical review board (TRB) is a project-level, decision-making body that must approve or disapprove all changes before they can be implemented. The CCB/TRB acts on changes that would cause material or substantive changes to the system, including design specifications, budget (including life cycle cost projections), project schedule, and interface characteristics with other systems, and the business model.

- Describe the project CCB/TRB, its roles and responsibilities, and its membership. The interaction between the CCB/TRB, project management, and management should also be presented in this section. If the CCB/TRB is divided into separate organizations, such as a main CCB/TRB, a software management board, or a technical review board, indicate such in your plan. Identify the roles and responsibilities, participants, and interaction between each group, project management, and business management.
- In addition, describe the SCM organizational requirements and how you meet those requirements, as well as the relationship to other project entities and management. Present the roles and responsibilities of each organization, and management area(s) within each business unit that will affect the SCM function.

Configuration Items

Configuration items (CIs) are the products that are to be placed under configuration control. A complete database that shows each item should be maintained for the funded and managed items by portfolio and should take into consideration the following:

- Management documentation describing the processes used to develop (or manage the development of) the system, such as the needs statement and the project plan (developed according to stakeholders, business, and management standards and procedures)
- Technical documentation or baselines describing the system that includes the security configuration (e.g., functional requirements document)
- Software components (computer programs, operating systems, and support tools)
- Data and database components (files and records that exist apart from software, which access the contents of a database)
- Network components (if applicable)
- Hardware components (computer workstations, peripherals, servers and routers, if applicable)
- Other components that management may wish to include at its discretion

Baseline Identification

A baseline is a collection of information describing the technical characteristics of each CI. Baselines serve as technical control points in the life cycle for the evaluation of proposed changes to these technical characteristics. The baseline and the approved changes or modifications provide a current description of the system. Using pictures to identify the systems assists management during the inventory process. When developing your SCMP you should include the following:

- Description of each system baseline, identified below, and the process by which it will be established and managed. This should include, but is not limited to, the physical contents of the baseline, including the code being developed, if applicable. The physical contents may include hard copies of documentation and commercial off-the-shelf (COTS) software. A graphic may also be created to depict where in the life cycle process each baseline is generated, and who becomes the responsible party of the identified baseline.

Functional Baseline

The functional baseline, sometimes called the requirements baseline, is the main product of the system definition phase and is managed in accordance with the functional requirements document and the data requirements document. It further identifies the security implications, risks, and mitigation steps taken within this phase to further define how the system will interact within the infrastructure.

- Include a subsection for software, hardware, interconnections, and documentation, including design documentation, as applicable.
- Describe where in the life cycle the functional baseline will be established, what security controls will be put in place, and the process by which it will be managed for the project and the infrastructure.

Design Baseline

The design baseline reflects activities performed during the system design phase. Its major component is a system/subsystem specification that defines the overall system design in terms of its subsystems, the allocation of requirements to subsystems, and interfaces between subsystems and interconnections. The user acceptance evaluation criteria component of this baseline is defined in the verification, validation, and test (VV&T) plan. The user acceptance evaluation criteria are not a separate document, but are a major element of the design baseline.

- Include a subsection for software and documentation, including design documentation, if applicable.

- Describe where in the life cycle the design baseline will be established and the process by which it will be managed for this project.

Development Baseline

The development baseline, generated during the system build phase, defines the detailed structure of the system being implemented. The development baseline's major components are the generation of the computer programs (code) and the database. Other components include training, users, operations, and maintenance documentation, in addition to the portfolio updates and management.

- Include a subsection for software, documentation, etc., as applicable.
- Describe where in the life cycle the development baseline will be established and the process by which it will be managed for this project.
- Provide any deviations from standards, exceptions to policy, or any specific requirements that affect the overall build of the system.
- Also provide program models used to develop software that is specific to the system.

Product Baseline

The product baseline is established during the system evaluation phase. The product baseline's major component is the end system product as built by the developers. This includes the following:

- Software
- Design and specification documentation
- Manuals (user, operations, maintenance, etc.)
- Installation and conversion procedures
- Software models
- Exceptions or deviations from standards

The product baseline is established after successful completion of the functional configuration audit (FCA), physical configuration audit (PCA), and associated system products and audit results presented at the system evaluation review. This baseline incorporates all changes needed to resolve problems detected during system acceptance and release testing, and any discrepancies identified between the system, its requirements, and design documentation.

> Functional configuration audit (FCA): Examines the functional characteristics of the configured product and verifies that the product has met, via test results, the requirements specified in its functional baseline documentation as approved by all stakeholders.
>
> Physical configuration audit (PCA): For each configuration item (CI), the formal comparison of a production-representative article with its design baseline to establish or verify the product baseline. For the system, the formal comparison of a production-representative system with its functional and design baselines, as well as any processes that apply at the system level, and the formal examination to confirm that the PCA was completed for each CI, that the decision database represents the system, that deficiencies discovered during testing have been resolved and changes approved, and that all approved changes have been implemented.

- Describe where in the life cycle the product baseline will be established, and the process by which it will be managed for this project.
- Identify the level of compliance the system meets, and whether or not the system is FCA and PCA compliant or what additional functions need to be met for compliance.

Roles and Responsibilities

Identify personnel who comprise the SCM group. The SCM group could vary from a single part-time individual to several full-time individuals. The size of the SCM group is dependent on a variety of factors, such as number of systems, system size, and system complexity. There should always be a stakeholder representative that can speak for the entire board as a point of contact within the group.

Personnel in the SCM group are identified below.

SCM MEMBER	CONTACT INFORMATION
[Name]	[Type of contact or specialty]
[Title]	[Full- or part-time]
[Department]	Phone: [XXX-XXX-XXXX]
	Email: XXX@yourcompany.net
[Name]	[Type of contact or specialty]
[Title]	[Full- or part-time]
[Department]	Phone: [XXX-XXX-XXXX]
	Email: XXX@yourcompany.net
[Name]	[Type of contact or specialty]
[Title]	[Full- or part-time]
[Department]	Phone: [XXX-XXX-XXXX]
	Email: XXX@yourcompany.net

Change Control Process

Change control provides a description of how requests for change or problem reports are initiated, processed, and completed. It also outlines security configuration management's role in life cycle reviews and audits, which are both formal mechanisms for establishing and reviewing project baselines.

Change Classifications

Classifying changes helps establish the priorities of change. This takes into account all personnel involved and helps establish a traceable process that ultimately documents the change to take place. Once you establish your priorities, make all attempts to stay with them. Sometimes it becomes difficult to place a change within any specific priority, and in this place, always escalate the priority to the next higher level, communicate your decision, and make every attempt to ensure a certain level of transparency in your processes.

As part of your plan describe how change classifications will be determined and assigned in terms of the level of severity of their impact. Selection factors may include

- Criticality: This can be a numeric system based on the department, business impact, and timeline you have to incorporate the change.

- Interface requirements: When a system interfaces with one or more systems change requirements must be decided that incorporate the entire interconnection and interface.
- Change sensitivity: Measured by the overall effect to the system, business model, and production process. How the system change affects each of these will vary and sensitivity will dictate scheduling.
- Maintenance schedule.
- Vendor schedule.
- Ownership.
- Scope and complexity.

Change Control Forms

Document the flow that generates how change control forms will be used from initiation through approval or disapproval. In addition, describe the forms that may be included in the change control process, such as

- Needs statement
- Requirements change
- Tracking options
- Approval process

Include sample forms in an appendix to this plan. These forms may include, but are limited to, problem reports, system change requests, impact analysis reports, and change authorization notices.

Problem Resolution Tracking

Describe the process used to log project problem requests and initiate resolution.

Measurements

Define the measurements used to determine the status of SCM activities, the effectiveness of SCM processes, and the stability of controlled baseline deliverables. These are more in line with the portfolio management activities, but it is good to have them in place for management questions and stakeholder inquiries.

Configuration Status Accounting

All SCM activities are recorded, stored, and reported by the configuration status accounting (CSA) function. The CSA function is a discipline that provides managers with feedback to determine whether decisions of the CCB/TRB are being implemented as directed. As approved changes are executed, the CSA function records and files data concerning the appropriately modified software, hardware, and documentation. The CSA function is responsible for identifying and issuing the most current approved versions of the SCM-controlled items to project participants.

Identify the format and contents of the status summary reports that will be produced by the CSA function, and include them in an appendix to this plan. Describe how the audit trail that identifies all changes implemented on approved baseline deliverables will be kept. Examples may include using hard copy, diskettes (hard or compact), or a COTS tool.

Outline the processes and describe how captured information will be used to accomplish functions such as assuring that the software meets the design intent, the contractual requirements are satisfied, and the tests are performed in accordance with test plans.

Configuration Management Libraries

For each library (development, pilot, production, etc.), describe the organization of the SCM library, including the multiple divisions of the library (the technical support library that stores the project development and production deliverables, the configuration library that contains records kept in support of the CCB/TRB, and the reference library consisting of technical documents that are either government produced or COTS). Each library type should be discussed in a separate subsection. You have to keep in mind that you are writing to stakeholders, and they need to understand how your organization is laid out and what data you are collecting. It is their approval that drives the progress!

Release Management (RM)

Discuss the means by which the release of all project CIs will be managed. In referring to RM, you need to define the process from inception, any development changes that are needed, man-hours in development for a specific project, and also what controls are in place to ensure that your release is the latest one.

Configuration Audits

Formal configuration audits are conducted at certain predetermined points as specified in the project plan. The purpose of the audit is to certify that the design, development, and integration meet the system's technical requirement, that they are accurately documented, and that they do not include unauthorized changes. With complex administrative systems, informal audits should be performed to minimize the impact on project schedules and identify deficiencies as soon as possible. Deficiencies noted during the informal audit, as well as recommendations for any corrective actions, are made available for CCB/TRB review during the configuration audit. Configuration audits validate compliance of development requirements by comparing the functioning system to its technical documentation.

Specify the type and number of audits to be conducted. This will be determined by the size and complexity of the project being undertaken. It will also determine if the audit is external or internal. Present how and when SCM will identify and conduct each functional and physical configuration audit.

Functional Configuration Audit

A functional configuration audit is a formal examination of test records to verify that functional characteristics of the system comply with its requirements.

Describe the process by which functional configuration audits will be performed.

Physical Configuration Audit

A physical configuration audit is a formal examination of each coded version of a configuration. It assesses the system's technical documentation for completeness and accuracy in describing the tested system and compares the tested system configuration with the operational system delivered to ensure the appropriate components are tested, and the system complies with all applicable standards. When reviewing the system be sure to include the following:

- Describe the process by which physical configuration audits will be performed.
- Identify deviations with the corporate policies.
- Include sign-off of key managers and stakeholders.
- Update document during any modifications.

Tools

List the software tools currently being used to support SCM activities. Identify tools used for library control, configuration inventory and change history, and status reporting. Also include any tools used by support maintenance personnel, software they may use to interact with the system or software, and the procedures that are used by the maintenance personnel. Some vendors have the tools and procedures listed within the support agreement; validate the support agreement each time that a support person interacts with the software and the system.

Training

The training describes SCM training requirements for all project personnel. All training should be documented within the individual's personal training folder or within the training records maintained by the organizational training coordinator. The training records should identify the training, the system trained, and the time spent on training, and if tested, the grade received.

Training supports costing when determining the return on investment (ROI) in deciding the overall cost advantage of the system.

Training Approach

Provide information regarding the content and scheduling of SCM training to be conducted for all personnel supporting the project. Train project personnel, including those assigned responsibility for performing SCM activities, in the objectives, procedures, and methods for performing their SCM-related duties. Examples of training include the following:

- Role, responsibility, and authority of the SCM personnel
- SCM standards, procedures, and methods
- Baselines of the system
- SCM tools and their capabilities
- Data measurement, analysis, and reporting

Security configuration management is not just a way to track a system through the life cycle; it incorporates all the industry best standards and requirements. SCM is configuration management (CM) with the incorporation of secure practices. An organization does not need to reinvent its procedures; it needs to train its personnel to start thinking in the secure configuration mind-set. Security is not just a process; it is a way of life, and in today's world a corporation cannot afford the loss of pertinent files, the embarrassment of defacement, or the leak of personnel data that can run in the millions. Think, eat, and drink secure configuration and the rewards are endless.

8

CONTINGENCY PLANNING

Contingency planning (CP) refers to interim measures to recover specific information technology systems within your infrastructure after a disruption, whereas a continuity of operations (COOP) plan refers to the corporate operations, personnel, and buildings. Interim measures of a CP may include relocation of information systems and operations to an alternate site, recovery of information system functions using alternate equipment, or performance of information system functions using manual methods.

This chapter provides strategies and techniques common to all systems and does not include COOP or disaster recovery (DR) procedures; although they may all relate to mission-critical information systems, the focus is planning for the IT infrastructure.

Contingency plans should be created after the system categorization, business impact analysis, risk assessment, and secure baseline configuration. The information gathered from those steps will assist you in completion of the appendixes for the business continuity plan (BCP).

NIST addresses seven steps in the contingency planning process; these steps are designed to be integrated into each stage of the system development life cycle (SDLC); therefore as you progress, you may find that there are many substeps to each process explained, and additional steps that you need to highlight in your specific plan. The National Institute of Standards and Technology (NIST) identifies the seven steps as

1. *Develop the contingency planning policy statement.* A formal policy provides the requirements, authority, and guidance necessary to develop an effective contingency plan. The policy should also define what testing/training procedures should be used and the time frame in which they are conducted and what standards you will be subjected to for a satisfactory rating or results. This also shows management buy-in of the program, which is critical to the existence of the program and continual support.

2. *Conduct the business impact analysis (BIA).* Within Chapter 5, we discuss the importance of the BIA and how it helps identify and prioritize information systems and components critical to supporting the corporate mission and business functions. A template for developing the BIA is provided to assist readers on the CRC Press website.

3. *Identify preventive controls.* These are steps taken by a system's administrator that ensure the reliability of operations and performance of an information system to provide its intended service within the business and mission functions that reduce the effects of system disruptions. Each step taken to increase the operational aspects will affect system availability and reduce contingency life cycle costs.

4. *Create contingency strategies.* Ben Franklin is quoted as saying, "An ounce of prevention is worth a pound of cure." How true when it comes to the operations and maintenance of an information technology infrastructure. Thorough recovery strategies ensure that the information system may be recovered quickly and effectively following a disruption.

5. *Develop an information system contingency plan.* The contingency plan should contain detailed guidance and procedures for restoring a system that specifies the restoration process unique to the system's security and business requirements. A British Army phrase states, "Prior proper planning prevents piss poor performance"; regardless of what adage you choose, you must develop a strategic and tactical process for all contingencies for recovery of your information systems. They should be tested quarterly, and testing can consist of any of the below items, depending on your budget:
   a. Table top
   b. Walk-through
   c. Contingency call-up
   d. Divisional/section/department
   e. Full-blown exercise

6. *Ensure plan testing, training, and exercises.* Testing validates recovery capabilities, whereas training prepares recovery personnel for plan activation, and exercising the plan identifies planning gaps; combined, the activities improve plan

effectiveness and overall preparedness. Management involvement in the test implants importance and buy-in from the management team. On either announced or unannounced tests, determining location is important when IT interfaces with management and "real" figures need to be identified to determine actual costs. Always add a buffer of 10% to 15% for unexpected events. During the testing process, explain the rules of the test during the initial brief, install injects into the exercise process to change the thought process of the players, and develop "what ifs" throughout the test to ensure the recovery team continues to think about all aspects of the recovery operations.

Figure 8.1 shows a flowchart of a test process that may assist you in developing your own procedures.

7. *Ensure plan maintenance.* Like everything we have been presenting within the book, the final phase is always some means of maintenance or monitoring. Everything you do is done better when you review it, have others review it, test it, and then maintain it! An after action review (AAR) is worth its weight in gold, and all levels of participants need to be

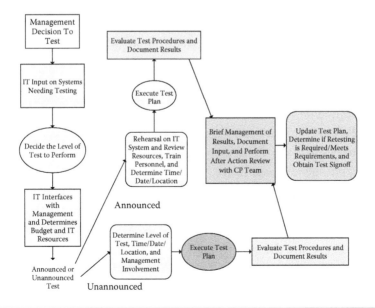

Figure 8.1   Business contingency plans flowchart.

present. A moderator or "test proctor" should be the overall coordinator, and not a person from the management team. Some people will not speak out if management leads; presence is important, but not as the test coordinator. Treat the CP as a living document that is updated, at a minimum of annually, so the document remains current with your system architecture enhancements and corporate manning changes. There is nothing worse than a plan put together in the past and a new person queries who that "unknown named person" is, and they left the company back in....

In addition to the one provided in the additional materials on the CRC Press website, NIST Special Publication 800-34, revision 1, on contingency planning presents three sample formats for developing an information system contingency plan. NIST plans are based on low-, moderate-, or high-impact level, and you will need to research what level of impact and security you wish to obtain. The Federal Information Processing Standard (FIPS) 199, *Standards for Security Categorization of Federal Information and Information Systems*, is a very good reference to assist you in what categories you place your IT systems. Each format defines three phases that govern actions to be taken following a system disruption. The guides are abundant starting points, and NIST deserves the accolades for taking the time to develop a template that is free to anyone that wishes to use it. The template format lays out the three phases:

1. **Activation/notification:** Describes the process of activating the plan based on outage impacts and notifying recovery personnel for the IT system.
2. **Recovery:** Details a suggested course of action for recovery teams to restore system operations at an alternate site or using contingency capabilities.
3. **Reconstitution:** Includes activities to test and validate system capability and functionality and outlines actions that can be taken to return the system to normal operating condition and prepare the system against future outages.

Because information system resources are so critical to an organization's success, it is pertinent that identified services provided by these systems are able to operate effectively without prolonged interruption—hence the purpose and validity of the business impact analysis (BIA). Contingency planning supports this requirement by establishing a top-down process that includes policy, procedures, thorough plans, and technical measures that can enable a system to be recovered as quickly and effectively as possible following a service disruption. Contingency planning is unique to each system, providing preventive measures, recovery strategies, and technical considerations appropriate to the system's information confidentiality, integrity, availability, and authentication requirements and the system impact level. In previous chapters I define the process of

1. Policy
2. Procedures
3. Test
4. Implementation
5. Maintenance

Your contingency planning falls into each one of those phases. The implementation and maintenance phases are used during and after the tests that ensure the plans work as designed. Information system contingency planning focuses on coordinated strategic management involving policy, procedures, and interaction with IT for the technical measures that enable the plans during a recovery of information systems, operations, and data after a disruption. Contingency planning includes one or more of the following approaches to restore disrupted services:

- Restoring information systems using alternate equipment:
  - Consider using your stored systems or a vendor that provides these services.
  - The services must identify priority of use for your company in the event of an actual requirement.
- Performing some or all of the affected business processes using alternate processing (manual) means (typically acceptable for only short-term disruptions):
  - System categorization is key to the recovery operations; all high-impact systems should be priority 1.
  - Recovery time/point objective (RTO/RPO) should be a second consideration; once you categorize the system you need to determine what system has more/less RTO.

- Recovering information systems operations at an alternate location (typically acceptable for only long-term disruptions or those physically impacting the facility):
  - Once again, the use of a vendor site might be more efficient and less costly.
- Implementing appropriate contingency planning controls based on the information system's security impact level:
  - This is primary to the RTO/RPO. This should also be based on the mission-essential functions and primary mission-essential functions (MEFs/PMEFs); although more related to the continuity of operations plans, it still must be considered in the contingency of the IT operational aspects.

The example plan in the additional materials provided on the CRC Press website and the NIST examples provide guidelines to individuals responsible for preparing and maintaining contingency plans (CPs). The document discusses essential contingency plan elements and processes and highlights specific considerations and concerns associated with contingency planning for all types of information system platforms, and provides tested examples to assist readers in developing their own CPs. When determining your plan and the information value, as determined by the stakeholders, management team, and technology team, it is essential to keep in mind and document for each information system the value based on

- **Maximum tolerable downtime (MTD):** The MTD represents the total amount of time the information system owner is willing to accept for a mission/business process outage or disruption and includes all impact considerations. Determining MTD is important because it could leave continuity planners with imprecise direction on
  - Selection of an appropriate recovery method
  - The depth of detail that will be required when developing recovery procedures, including their scope and content
- **Recovery time objective (RTO):** RTO defines the maximum amount of time that a system resource can remain unavailable before there is an unacceptable impact on other system resources, supported mission/business functions, and the MTD. Determining the information system resource

RTO is important for selecting appropriate technologies that are best suited for meeting the MTD.

- When it is not feasible to immediately meet the RTO and the MTD is inflexible, a plan of action and milestone should be initiated to document the situation and plan for its mitigation.

- **Recovery point objective (RPO):** The RPO represents the point in time, prior to a disruption or system outage, to which mission/business process data can be recovered (given the most recent backup copy of the data) after an outage. Because the RTO must ensure that the MTD is not exceeded, the RTO must normally be shorter than the MTD. For example, a system outage may prevent a particular process from being completed, and because it takes time to reprocess the data, that additional processing time must be added to the RTO to stay within the time limit established by the MTD.

While the principles and priorities of contingency planning establish a baseline to meet most needs, it is recognized that each company may have additional requirements specific to its own infrastructure. NIST guidance provides background information on interrelationships between information system contingency planning and other types of security and emergency management-related contingency plans, organizational resiliency, and the system development life cycle (SDLC). Together, they form a format for security as the baseline of the company and help define how the company can develop the infrastructure using security as its foundation and developing the remaining processes as by-products of the foundation, as explained throughout this book.

Using this book and the guidance of NIST, NIST SP 800-34 r1, NIST SP 800-37, NIST Special Publication 800-53, and FIPS 199, contingency planning and the associated security controls are designed into the security foundation of the company and integrated throughout the life cycle of the organizational development life cycles and build on the foundation and by-products of your infrastructure. In consideration of the three impact levels, it is recommended that you use FIPS 199 and FIPS 200; they keep it simple and the levels are understood throughout the industry.

Just ensure you develop good functional boundaries for each system, as discussed in previous chapters, and also defined within NIST SP 800-37. When using the recommended impact levels and associated security controls in developing your infrastructure, the appropriate contingency planning strategic objectives will provide your company with a very thorough and complete guide in obtaining the company goals in CP.

Here the planning principles, which can be used for a wide variety of situations, affect information system operations that can be implemented for short-term disruptions to disasters that affect normal operations for an extended period. Contingency planning does not replace disaster recovery (DR) or contingency of operations plans (COOP); it supplements them. Understand that there is a difference between the types of recovery operations; although similar in functions and procedures, CP deals with each specific system. Your DRP and COOP plan will address continuity of mission/business functions. Although information systems typically support mission/business functions, the functions also depend on a variety of other resources and capabilities not associated with information systems. Recovery of mission-essential functions (MEFs) is addressed by COOP plans or business continuity plans (BCPs). The COOP and DR plans are part of security and emergency management-related plans, and further guidance can be obtained through the Federal Emergency Management Agency (FEMA) website or as discussed in NIST SP 800-34.

The level of responsibility for a complete and effective plan starts from the top down, and their responsibilities include the following:

- *Chief information officers* (CIOs), with overall responsibility for the organization's information systems and management of the staff, collect metrics from CISOs and provide to stakeholders.
- *Managers* are responsible for overseeing information system operations or mission/business functions that rely on information systems.
- *Corporate information security officers* (CISOs) are responsible for interacting with stakeholders and developing and maintaining the security of information systems at the organizational level. They provide oversight to the ISSO and ISSM (IAO/IAM).

- *Information system security officers* (ISSOs)/*information system security managers* (ISSMs) and other staff are responsible for developing, implementing, and maintaining an information system's security activities, and providing input to CISOs for policy and procedure development. They are also referred to as information assurance officers (IAOs) and information assurance managers (IAMs).
- *System engineers and architects* are responsible for designing, implementing, or modifying information systems, documenting the system development life cycle (SDLC) throughout the entire life cycle of technical changes, and interacting with the configuration control board/technical review board (CCB/TRB).
- *System administrators* are responsible for maintaining daily information system operations.
- *Users* employ desktop and portable systems to perform their assigned job functions.

This chapter is provided to lead the reader through the contingency plan development process. The process includes designing a contingency planning program, a management responsibility that evaluates the organization's needs against contingency strategy options input from the technology personnel that are based on the system impact levels, security controls, and technical considerations, and then documenting the contingency strategy into a contingency plan, testing the plan, and maintaining it. The resulting contingency plan serves as a "user's manual" for executing the strategy in the event of a disruption and should be written at a level that can be performed by almost anyone.

- **Contingency planning process:** Details the basic planning principles necessary for developing an effective contingency capability within the company. The principles outlined are applicable to all information systems. This chapter presents contingency planning guidelines for all elements of the planning cycle, including business impact analysis, alternate site selection, and recovery strategies. This chapter and the example available on the CRC Press website also discuss the development of contingency plan teams and the roles and responsibilities commonly assigned to personnel during plan activation.

- **Contingency plan development:** Breaks down the activities necessary to document the information system contingency strategy and develop the CP. Maintaining, testing, training, and exercising the contingency plan are also discussed.
- **Technical contingency planning considerations:** Describe contingency planning concerns specific to the platform types to help contingency planners identify, select, and implement the appropriate technical contingency measures for their given systems.

An organization must have the ability to withstand all hazards and sustain its mission through environmental changes; the situations of Hurricane Katrina and the Twin Towers would have posed different outcomes (technically) if they each had a working CP in place. Changes can be gradual, such as economic or mission changes, or sudden, as in a disaster event. Rather than just working to identify and mitigate threats, vulnerabilities, and risks, organizations can work toward building a resilient infrastructure, minimizing the impact of any disruption on mission-essential functions.

Your company needs to keep a flexible posture so you can quickly adapt and recover from any type of changes to the IT infrastructure, and this is started by a thorough and practiced response posture. Maintaining flexibility is not a procedure you can document, but rather an end state for your organization to reach by quality practice and sound developed continuity operations. The additional information available on the CRC Press website contains an Excel workbook titled "FCD 2 Attachment_A_MEF-PMEF_Workbook_02-2008.xls," which can give you a starting point for documenting your company's MEF/PMEFs. An additional reference through FEMA (FCD2) is also provided and can be adapted to fit your situation. The goal of a resilient organization is to continue mission-essential functions and primary mission-essential functions at all times during any type of disruption. Companies that continually strive for flexibility and work to adapt to changes and risks that are probable or possible threats will allow you to continue critical and primary mission-essential functions. Risk management, contingency, and continuity planning are individual security and emergency management activities that can help you build a secure foundation and can also be implemented in a holistic manner across the company as components of a resilient IT infrastructure sustainability program.

Effective contingency planning begins with the development of an organization process of documentation, as previously defined, training, and complementing the procedures and documents with a contingency planning policy for each information system. This facilitates prioritizing the systems, and a process based on policy, procedures, implementation, testing, and monitoring strengthens the development of the priorities established for the company recovery strategies and minimizes loss. Following sound and secure infrastructure development processes assists the company in maintaining a future market and helps to build on the four security objectives: confidentiality, integrity, availability, and authentication (CIAA). NIST uses the three security objectives and defines CIA. I believe that adding the fourth A, authentication, builds a more secure foundation and also keeps it in the forefront of the development process of building security principles.

- *Confidentiality* preserves authorized restrictions on information access and disclosure, including means for protecting personal privacy and proprietary information.
- *Integrity* guards against improper information modification or destruction, and includes ensuring information nonrepudiation and authenticity.
- *Availability* ensures timely and reliable access to and use of information.
- *Authentication* ensures that the information systems are accessed by persons with a need to know and authority to use the information system. This goes beyond the username/password and uses a more positive physical means, like biometrics.
  - Something you know: Something you mentally possess, this could be a password, a secret word known by the user.
  - Something you have: Any form of issued self-identification:
    - SecurID
    - CryptoCard
    - Activcard
    - SafeWord
    - Many other forms of identification

- Something you are: A physical characteristic, such as voice, fingerprint, iris pattern, and other biometric devices.

Contingency planning considerations and strategies address the impact level of the confidentiality, integrity, availability, and authentication of your security objective for information systems. Strategies for high-impact information systems should consider high confidentiality, integrity, availability, and authentication and redundancy options in their design. Options may include the following:

- Fully redundant load-balanced systems at alternate sites
- Data mirroring
- Off-site database replication

High-availability information systems are the information systems that should be addressed as your mission-essential functions. Contingencies for these systems are normally expensive to set up, operate, and maintain and should be considered only for those high-impact information systems categorized with a high confidentiality, integrity, availability, and authentication security objective. Lower-impact information systems may be able to use less expensive contingency options and should tolerate longer downtimes for recovery or restoration of data. As addressed, determining the level of confidentiality, integrity, availability, and authentication is critical to addressing the information system and placing it into a category that defines its mission. Each of the areas of a system must be explored, and if you choose to use a "high water mark" for the classification of the system, then consider everything that applies to the overall impact level of that system. This is covered more clearly in Chapter 4, and FIPS 199/200 should be used to determine the overall impact on the information system. There is an additional reference on the federal level under NIST SP 800-60 that identifies the types of system and impact they may pose on a national level. These are guides, but your information systems can be compared to what is listed. Nothing beats time and experience with your company, so your best judgment plays an important role in the final determination, along with input from the management team and stockholders.

Using a solid system development life cycle in building your contingency plans includes incorporating security controls similar to those developed in NIST SP 800-53 early in the development of an information system, and maintaining these controls on an ongoing basis. Within the family of contingency planning, NIST SP 800-53, revision 3, identifies 10 security controls for your information systems that will help guide you through the selection process and determine what security controls are needed for the impact level of your system. Not all controls are applicable to all systems. The FIPS 199 security categorization determines which controls apply to a particular system. For example, information systems that have availability as a security objective categorized as low impact do not require alternate processing or storage sites, and information systems that have an availability security objective categorized as moderate impact require compliance with only the first system backup control enhancements. Using the FIPS 199 security categorization allows for tailoring of the CP security controls in NIST SP 800-53 to those applicable to the appropriate security control baselines.

As shown in Chapter 4, the formula below can be used to help document the decision process and impact level of your information system. When documenting the decision you should include a narrative for each impact decision for future reference. These documents should be, at least, classified as company sensitive and not releasable to outside sources. The formula is

Security category information system = {(confidentiality, impact), (integrity, impact), (availability, impact), (authentication, impact)}

Decision justification:

- **Confidentiality:** The impact level of confidentiality is determined to be H, M, L because the system functions as a {domain controller, financial records store, database, web server}, and in support of the system requirements it has been determined to be a {mission-essential function, non-mission-essential function} system by the {stakeholders, CIO management team, etc.}. The information system {does/does not} contain personally identifiable information (PII) or other mission/business-sensitive data.
- **Integrity:** The impact level of integrity is determined to be H, M, L because the system functions as a {domain controller, financial records store, database, web server}, and in support of the system requirements it has been determined to be

a {mission-essential function, non-mission-essential function} system by the {stakeholders, CIO management team, etc.}. The information system {does/does not} contain mission/business-sensitive information.

- **Availability:** The impact level of availability is determined to be H, M, L because the system functions as a {domain controller, financial records store, web server}, and in support of the system requirements it has been determined to be a {mission-essential function, non-mission-essential function} system by the {stakeholders, CIO management team, etc.}. The system {does/does not} contain information that requires {immediate, up-to-date} usage.

- **Authentication:** The impact level of authentication is determined to be H, M, L because the system functions as a {domain controller, financial records store, database, web server}, and in support of the system requirements it has been determined to be a {mission-essential function, non-mission-essential function} system by the {stakeholders, CIO management team, etc.}. The system authentication requirements {are/are not} restricted to {internal/external} access and strict authentication requirements {are/are not} required.

Within NIST SP 800-53, it identifies the control guidelines as shown and is provided as an example on how to document what controls are required by your organization for implementation. The contingency planning controls are shown for all three impact levels, H, M, L, if you choose to use them. CP-5, contingency plan update, does not show as applicable but is a best practice to apply and update on, at least, an annual basis. Do not wait until you have an exercise; the exercise is used to test your documented procedures (Table 8.1).

Types of Plans

NIST has spent exhaustive hours developing standards and procedures for information systems; the following information is provided by it and included within NIST SP 800-34, these are free resources that apply to any information system or organization, anywhere (Table 8.2).

Table 8.1 NIST SP 800-53 Contingency Planning Controls for Low, Moderate, and High Impact

CONTROL NO.	CONTROL NAME	SECURITY CONTROL BASELINES		
		LOW	MODERATE	HIGH
CP-1	Contingency Planning Policy and Procedures	CP-1	CP-1	CP-1
CP-2	Contingency Plan	CP-2	CP-2 (1)	CP-2 (1) (2) (3)
CP-3	Contingency Training	CP-3	CP-3	CP-3 (1)
CP-4	Contingency Plan Testing and Exercise	CP-4	CP-4 (1)	CP-4 (1) (2) (4)
CP-5	Contingency Plan Update (Withdrawn)	—	—	—
CP-6	Alternate Storage Site	Not selected	CP-6 (1) (3)	CP-6 (1) (2) (3)
CP-7	Alternate Processing Site	Not selected	CP-7 (1) (2) (3) (5)	CP-7 (1) (2) (3) (4) (5)
CP-8	Telecommunications Services	Not selected	CP-8 (1) (2)	CP-8 (1) (2) (3) (4)
CP-9	Information System Backup	CP-9	CP-9 (1)	CP-9 (1) (2) (3)
CP-10	Information System Recovery and Reconstitution	CP-10	CP-10 (2) (3)	CP-10 (2) (3) (4)

Information system contingency planning represents a broad scope of activities designed to sustain and recover critical system services following an emergency event. Information system contingency planning fits into a much broader security and emergency management effort that includes organizational and business process continuity, disaster recovery planning, and incident management. Ultimately, an organization would use a suite of plans to properly prepare response, recovery, and continuity activities for disruptions affecting the organization's information systems, mission/business functions, personnel, and the facility. Because there is an inherent relationship between an information system and the mission/business process it supports, there must be coordination between each plan during development and updates to ensure that recovery strategies and supporting resources neither negate each other nor duplicate efforts.

Continuity and contingency planning are critical components of emergency management and organizational resilience but are often confused in their use.

Table 8.2 Types of Plans

PLAN	PURPOSE	SCOPE	PLAN RELATIONSHIP
Business continuity plan (BCP)	Provides procedures for sustaining mission/business operations while recovering from a significant disruption	Addresses mission/business functions at a lower or expanded level from COOP mission-essential functions	Mission/business process-focused plan that may be activated in coordination with a COOP plan to sustain non–mission-essential functions
Continuity of operations (COOP) plan	Provides procedures and guidance to sustain an organization's mission-essential functions at an alternate site for up to 30 days; mandated by federal directives	Addresses mission-essential functions at a facility; information systems are addressed based only on their support of the mission-essential functions	MEF-focused plan that may also activate several business unit-level BCPs, CPs, or DRPs, as appropriate
Cyber incident response plan	Provides procedures for mitigating and correcting a cyber-attack, such as a virus, worm, or Trojan horse	Addresses mitigation and isolation of affected systems, cleanup, and minimizing loss of information	Information system-focused plan that may activate a CP or DRP, depending on the extent of the attack or impact on the infrastructure
Disaster recovery plan (DRP)	Provides procedures for relocating information systems operations to an alternate location	Activated after major system disruptions with long-term effects	Information system-focused plan that activates one or more CPs for recovery of individual systems
Information system contingency plan (CP)	Provides procedures and capabilities for recovering an information system	Addresses single information system recovery at the current or, if appropriate, alternate location	Information system-focused plan that may be activated independent of other plans or as part of a larger recovery effort coordinated with a DRP, COOP, or BCP
Occupant emergency plan (OEP)	Provides coordinated procedures for minimizing loss of life or injury and protecting property damage in response to a physical threat	Focuses on personnel and property particular to the specific facility; not mission/business process or information system based	Incident-based plan that is initiated immediately after an event, preceding a COOP or DRP activation
Crisis communications plan	Provides procedures for disseminating internal and external communications; means to provide critical status information and control rumors	Addresses communications with personnel and the public; not information system focused	Incident-based plan often activated with a COOP or BCP, but may be used alone during a public exposure event

- *Continuity planning* normally applies to the mission/business itself; it concerns the ability to continue critical functions and processes during and after an emergency event.
- *Contingency planning* normally applies to information systems, and provides the steps needed to recover the operation of all or part of designated information systems at an existing or new location in an emergency.
- *Cyber incident response planning* is a type of plan that normally focuses on detection, response, and recovery to a computer security incident or event.

In general, universally accepted definitions for information system contingency planning and the related planning areas have not been available. Occasionally, this leads to confusion regarding the actual scope and purpose of various types of plans. To provide a common basis of understanding regarding information system contingency planning, this section identifies several other types of plans and describes their purpose and scope relative to information system contingency planning. Because of the lack of standard definitions for these types of plans, the scope of actual plans developed by organizations may vary from the following descriptions. This guide applies the descriptions and references in sections below to security and emergency management-related plans.

Business Continuity Plan (BCP)

The BCP focuses on sustaining an organization's mission/business functions during and after a disruption. An example of a mission/business function may be an organization's payroll process or customer service process. A BCP may be written for mission/business functions within a single business unit or may address the entire organization's processes. The BCP may also be scoped to address only the functions deemed to be priorities. A BCP may be used for long-term recovery in conjunction with the COOP plan, allowing for additional functions to come online as resources or time allow. Because mission/business functions use information systems, the business continuity planner must coordinate with information system owners to ensure that the BCP expectations and information system capabilities are matched.

Continuity of Operations (COOP) Plan

The COOP plan focuses on restoring an organization's mission-essential functions (MEFs) at an alternate site and performing those functions for up to 30 days before returning to normal operations. Additional functions, or those at a field office level, may be addressed by a BCP. Minor threats or disruptions that do not require relocation to an alternate site are typically not addressed in a COOP plan.

Standard elements of a COOP plan include the following:

Program plans and procedures	Continuity communications
Risk management	Vital records management
Budgeting and acquisition of resources	Human capital
Essential functions	Test, training, and exercise
Order of succession	Devolution
Delegation of authority	Reconstitution
Continuity facilities	

Cyber Incident Response Plan

The cyber incident response plan establishes procedures to address cyber-attacks against an organization's information system(s). These procedures are designed to enable security personnel to identify, mitigate, and recover from malicious computer incidents, such as unauthorized access to a system or data, denial of service, or unauthorized changes to system hardware, software, or data (e.g., malicious logic, such as a virus, worm, or Trojan horse). This plan may be included as an appendix of the BCP.

Disaster Recovery Plan (DRP)

The DRP applies to major, usually physical, disruptions to service that deny access to the primary facility infrastructure for an extended period. A DRP is an information system-focused plan designed to restore operability of the target system, application, or computer facility infrastructure at an alternate site after an emergency. The DRP may be supported by multiple information system contingency plans to address recovery of impacted individual systems once the alternate facility has been established. A DRP may support a BCP or COOP plan by recovering supporting systems for mission/ business functions or mission-essential functions at an alternate location. The DRP only addresses information system disruptions that require relocation.

Contingency Plan (CP)

A CP provides established procedures for the assessment and recovery of a system following a system disruption. The CP provides key information needed for system recovery, including roles and responsibilities, inventory information, assessment procedures, detailed recovery procedures, and testing of a system.

The CP differs from a DRP primarily in that the information system contingency plan procedures are developed for recovery of the system regardless of site or location. A CP can be activated at the system's current location or at an alternate site. In contrast, a DRP is primarily a site-specific plan developed with procedures to move operations of one or more information systems from a damaged or uninhabitable location to a temporary alternate location. Once the DRP has successfully transferred an information system site to an alternate site, each affected system would then use its respective information system contingency plan to restore, recover, and test systems, and put them into operation.

Occupant Emergency Plan (OEP)

The OEP outlines first-response procedures for occupants of a facility in the event of a threat or incident to the health and safety of personnel, the environment, or property. Such events include a fire, bomb threat, chemical release, domestic violence in the workplace, or a medical emergency. Shelter-in-place procedures for events requiring personnel to stay inside the building rather than evacuate are also addressed in an OEP. OEPs are developed at the facility level, specific to the geographic location and structural design of the building. The facility OEP may be appended to the COOP or BCP, but is executed separately and as a first response to the incident.

Ensure that you coordinate with your local response centers to ensure that your OEP is consistent with what has been designed. It is good practice to have your evacuation routes coordinate with those as addressed in the metropolis in which you exist. It is also good practice to have "ready kits" for first aid, communications, and food and water in the event the response team needs to remain on-site.

Crisis Communications Plan

Organizations should document standard procedures for internal and external communications in the event of a disruption using a crisis communications plan. A crisis communications plan is often developed by the organization responsible for public outreach. The plan provides various formats for communications appropriate to the incident. The crisis communications plan typically designates specific individuals as the *only* authority for answering questions from or providing information to the public regarding emergency response. It may also include procedures for disseminating reports to personnel on the status of the incident and templates for public press releases. The crisis communication plan procedures should be communicated to the organization's COOP and BCP planners to ensure that the plans include clear direction that only approved statements are released to the public by authorized officials.

Backup Methods and Off-Site Storage

System data should be backed up regularly. Policies should specify the minimum frequency of backups (e.g., daily or weekly, incremental or full) based on data criticality and the frequency that new information is introduced. Data backup policies should designate the location of stored data, file-naming conventions, media rotation frequency, and method for transporting data off-site. Data may be backed up on magnetic disk, tape, or optical disks, such as compact disks (CDs). The specific method chosen for conducting backups should be based on system and data availability and integrity requirements. These methods may include electronic vaulting, network storage, and tape library systems (Table 8.3).

Table 8.3 Categories of Backup and Media

FIPS 199 AVAILABILITY IMPACT LEVEL	INFORMATION SYSTEM TARGET PRIORITY AND RECOVERY	BACKUP/RECOVERY STRATEGY
Low	Low priority—any outage with little impact, damage, or disruption to the organization	Backup: Tape backup Strategy: Relocate or cold site
Moderate	Important or moderate priority—any system that, if disrupted, would cause a moderate problem to the organization and possibly other networks or systems	Backup: Optical backup, wide area network/virtual local area network (WAN/VLAN) replication, and virtual tape Strategy: Cold or warm site
High	Mission critical or high priority—damage or disruption to these systems would cause the most impact on the organization, mission, and other networks and systems	Backup: Mirrored systems, disk replication, and virtual tape Strategy: Hot site

It is good business practice to store backed-up data off-site, outside the threat area you are in and at least 5 miles away. Commercial data storage facilities are specially designed to archive media and protect data from threatening elements. If using off-site storage, data are backed up at the organization's facility and then labeled, packed, and transported to the storage facility. If the data are required for recovery or testing purposes, the organization contacts the storage facility requesting specific data to be transported to the organization or to an alternate facility.

Commercial storage facilities often offer media transportation and response and recovery services.

When selecting an off-site storage facility and vendor, the following criteria should be considered:

- **Priority of use:** Ensure the contract between your company and the vendor identifies a priority of use clause and that your organization has the priority level needed for your recovery.
- **Geographic area:** Distance from the organization and the probability of the storage site being affected by the same disaster as the organization's primary site.
- **Accessibility:** Length of time necessary to retrieve the data from storage and the storage facility's operating hours.
- **Security:** Security capabilities of the shipping method, storage facility, and personnel; all must meet the data's security requirements.

- **Environment:** Structural and environmental conditions of the storage facility (i.e., temperature, humidity, fire prevention, and power management controls).
- **Cost:** Cost of shipping, operational fees, and disaster response/recovery services.

Contingency planning is essential in today's business structures, as learned through Hurricane Katrina and the attack on the World Trade Center, for example. Many businesses were not able to recover due to the lack of tried, tested, and maintained contingency planning procedures. Don't become victim to procrastination. Cost-effective plans and procedures can be developed through the use of NIST documentation, which is available at the NIST Computer Security Division Resource Center: http://csrc.nist.gov/publications/PubsSPs.html.

9
Cloud Computing

Cloud computing is not new. Back in the 1950s various educational institutions used it to share processing power, and from there the Advanced Research Projects Agency Network (ARPANET) was developed and came to be the world's first operational packet switching network, later renamed Defense Advanced Research Projects Agency (DARPA). From all this derived MILNET, now known as NIPRNET, and what marketing has coined "the cloud," a collection of servers that perform application processing to storage of a company's data. The cloud is arranged in one of four configurations from a private site of hosted information systems to a hybrid site consisting of multiple arrangements.

Hackers are not new either. From the first Internet connection using dial-up modems, as depicted in a book, later made into a movie, *The Cuckoo's Egg: Tracking a Spy through the Maze of Computer Espionage*, that was based on a few-cent error in accounting, we have grown into state and freelance groups that have a need to gain access and destroy or steal your data. Using security as your model in all your computing needs is essential in the information age of our technological growth.

Cloud computing isn't cheap. Most studies dating back to 2009 have about a one-third increase in the cost of cloud computing over a private cloud scenario. You still have to maintain the cost of personnel, maintenance, infrastructure, and security, to name a few factors. Okay, you might save a little on security, but then you are transferring the responsibility, not the overall requirements—you need to consider what is currently in place within your own infrastructure and transfer that to a service level agreement.

Current-day technologies, industrial espionage, sharing of information, the amount of information, data storage archives, and the need for processing power and the ability to communicate over long distance created the need for infrastructure security, but few have ever used security as a model, and it was laid to rest in a series of books called "The Rainbow Series." From this we have come into the information age to find that many models exist, and they all want a lot of money to implement. Cost-effective computing does not come from buying the newest widget; it comes from the application of sound policy, procedures, and practices. Through Executive Order and Public Law 107-347, the National Institute of Standards and Technology (NIST) has developed sound industry practices using cost-effective computing.

I use NIST as a reference for the majority of my work not only due to the unbiased opinion and work performed, but also because it spends countless hours doing the research and practice to ensure that organizations have simple and understandable methods to follow. I commend NIST on the amount of time and depth of view it provides and makes available to all levels of the business market.

Most organizations tend to spend a small amount on security, and security professionals lack the overall knowledge due to inexperience or lack of guidance. NIST provides free publications to the industry; most people do not take advantage of it but should. In a survey conducted by the Enterprise Strategy Group (ESG) in January 2012, it stated, "More than half of organizations expect to increase their information security spending in 2012, some by 8% or more." This survey, coupled with a *CIO Journal* survey, is a main reason for an organization to get on line with cost-effective computing and the use of NIST. In September 2012 the *CIO Journal* posted a survey conducted by PricewaterhouseCoopers (PwC), "Companies Trim IT Security as Budgets Stagnate," that stated, "The cutbacks have occurred as the growth of security budgets has slowed, according to a new study from PricewaterhouseCoopers, which surveyed 9,300 CIOs, CEOS and IT managers on their preparedness for hacker attacks." With the cuts in security and the costs of cloud computing, it makes sense that a company would have the desire to implement a cost savings across the board and implement cost-effective computing. Although the desire does still remain and it seems the "correct way to improve," the cloud moves forward.

Cloud computing is not complex; overall, it is merely a place that has very powerful servers that provide a place to store or run applications, and from that it provides a central point of redundant communications. Cloud computing allows an organization to shift responsibility and some costs over to a provider. The service level agreements and level of security afforded by the provider must be defined in the agreements.

Applying security controls to a cloud, or the requirements of application security, is something that you must still be familiar with and enforce on your systems. Application of a cloud environment is a strategic mission/business decision that must not be taken lightly. You still remain responsible for the recovery and backup, regardless of how it is defined within your service agreement.

The National Institute of Standards and Technology has created a series of publications, and I found NIST SP 800-146, *Cloud Computing Synopsis and Recommendations*, to be the most extensive to date on all considerations of use, security, and models of the cloud computing environment. NIST SP 800-145 identifies cloud computing as follows:

> Cloud Computing is merely a model for enabling convenient, on-demand network access to shared data pool(s) of configurable computing resources (e.g., networks, servers, storage, applications, and services) that can be rapidly provisioned and released with minimal management effort or service provider interaction.

Cloud computing models include the following:

1. *Consume* refers to the network and connected infrastructure. This relates to the following essential characteristics:
   - On-demand self-service
   - Broad network access
   - Resource pooling
   - Rapid elasticity
   - Measured service

2. *Build* is defined within the services, and a model of the entire infrastructure is provisioned as defined by the client's needs. There are three service models:

   - Cloud software as a service (SaaS)
   - Cloud platform as a service (PaaS)
   - Cloud infrastructure as a service (IaaS)

3. *Hosting* is determined by how much you want to share. Some of the models to choose from include the following:
    - Private cloud: A private cloud is a cloud of information systems built on your own hardware and software or that of the provider.
    - Community cloud: Generally a group of users that have the same infrastructure requirements and standards.
    - Public cloud: Shared resources billed by use over a time frame as agreed with the service provider.
    - Hybrid cloud: A combination of any of the above.

Key enabling technologies include

- Fast wide area networks
- Powerful, inexpensive server computers
- High-performance virtualization for commodity hardware

The cloud computing model offers the promise of massive cost savings combined with increased IT agility, depending on what survey you read. It is considered critical that government and industry begin adoption of this technology in response to difficult economic constraints. However, cloud computing technology challenges many traditional approaches to data center and enterprise application design and management. Cloud computing is currently being used; however, security, interoperability, and portability are cited as major barriers to broader adoption.

The long-term goal is to provide thought leadership and guidance around the cloud computing archetype to catalyze its use within industry and government. NIST aims to shorten the adoption cycle, which will enable near-term cost savings and an increased ability to quickly create and deploy enterprise applications. NIST aims to foster cloud computing systems and practices that support interoperability, portability, and security requirements that are appropriate and achievable for important usage scenarios.

Essential Characteristics

On-demand self-service: A consumer can unilaterally provision computing capabilities, such as server time and network storage, as needed automatically without requiring human interaction with each service's provider.

Broad network access: Capabilities are available over the network and accessed through standard mechanisms that promote use by heterogeneous thin or thick client platforms (e.g. mobile phones, laptops, and PDAs).

Resource pooling: The provider's computing resources are pooled to serve multiple consumers using a multitenant model, with different physical and virtual resources dynamically assigned and reassigned according to consumer demand. There is a sense of location independence in that the customer generally has no control or knowledge over the exact location of the provided resources but may be able to specify location at a higher level of abstraction (e.g., country, state, or data center). Examples of resources include storage, processing, memory, network bandwidth, and virtual machines.

Rapid elasticity: Capabilities can be rapidly and elastically provisioned, in some cases automatically, to quickly scale out, and rapidly released to quickly scale in. To the consumer, the capabilities available for provisioning often appear to be unlimited and can be purchased in any quantity at any time.

Measured service: Cloud systems automatically control and optimize resource use by leveraging a metering capability at some level of abstraction appropriate to the type of service (e.g., storage, processing, bandwidth, and active user accounts). Resource usage can be monitored, controlled, and reported, providing transparency for both the provider and consumer of the utilized service.

Service Models

Cloud software as a service (SaaS): The capability provided to the consumer is to use the provider's applications running on a cloud infrastructure. The applications are accessible from various client devices through a thin client interface such as a web browser (e.g., web-based email). The consumer does not manage or control the underlying cloud infrastructure, including network, servers, operating systems, storage, or even individual application capabilities, with the possible exception of limited user-specific application configuration settings.

Cloud platform as a service (PaaS): The capability provided to the consumer is to deploy onto the cloud infrastructure consumer or acquired applications created using programming languages and tools supported by the provider. The consumer does not manage or control the underlying cloud infrastructure, including network, servers, operating systems, or storage, but has control over the deployed applications and possibly application hosting environment configurations.

Cloud infrastructure as a service (IaaS): The capability provided to the consumer is to provision processing, storage, networks, and other fundamental computing resources where the consumer is able to deploy and run arbitrary software, which can include operating systems and applications. The consumer does not manage or control the underlying cloud infrastructure but has control over operating systems, storage, deployed applications, and possibly limited control of select networking components (e.g., host firewalls).

Implementing the cloud environment for your organization is a cost and responsibility issue. There are many resources that identify the pros and cons of cloud computing. In the event that your company has intentions, present the facts to what the current cost of the information technology environment is and get some hard figures as to what it will be. A cost-benefit analysis is a good start.

In addition, you need to look at what level of monitoring the vendor does and what additional packages are delivered at what cost. What level of security is offered? What certifications does the vendor have? What additional costs are to be applied if your security level is different?

10

CONTINUOUS MONITORING

Continuous monitoring is an effort that is exercised throughout the infrastructure and is led by management and reflected within an organization's mission-critical functions. These functions have become dependent upon information technology; the ability to manage this technology and guarantee confidentiality, integrity, availability, and authentication of information is now also mission critical. In designing the enterprise architecture and corresponding security architecture, an organization seeks to securely meet the IT infrastructure needs of its stakeholders, mission, and core business processes. Information security is a dynamic process that must be effectively and proactively managed for an organization to identify and respond to new vulnerabilities, evolving threats, and an organization's constantly changing enterprise architecture, manning, and operational environment.

Any effort or process intended to support ongoing monitoring of information security across an organization begins with leadership defining a comprehensive continuous monitoring strategy encompassing personnel, technology, processes, procedures, and operating environments. This definitive and flexible strategy

- Is grounded in a clear understanding of the organization's ability to respond to risk and helps management set priorities and manage risk consistently throughout the organization
- Includes metrics that provide direction, meaning, and is symptomatic of the security status at all organizational tiers
- Ensures continued effectiveness of all security controls that encompass the information technology systems, personnel, and business objectives
- Verifies compliance with information security requirements derived from organizational mission/business functions, corporate directives, regulations, policies, and standards/ guidelines

- Is informed by all organizational IT assets and helps to maintain visibility in the security of the assets
- Builds its metrics from trends and trend analysis of data that have been determined to be essential to the business model, threats, and vulnerabilities
- Ensures knowledge and control of changes to organizational systems and environments of operation
- Maintains awareness of threats and vulnerabilities, cost-effective computing, and mitigation procedures

A continuous monitoring program is established to collect information in accordance with preestablished metrics, utilizing information readily available in part through implemented security controls and sound practices within the information technology infrastructure security requirements.

Organizations collect and analyze the data regularly and as often as needed to manage risk as appropriate for each organizational tier. This process involves the entire organization, from senior leaders providing governance and strategic vision to individuals developing, implementing, and operating individual systems in support of the organization's core missions and business processes. Subsequently, determinations are made from an organizational perspective on whether to conduct mitigation activities or to reject, transfer, or accept risk. Regardless, management has applied due diligence and due care in the decision process and consulted with the security staff on what procedures best suit the organizational security posture. Application of the tier levels considers all aspects of the organization and their corresponding levels:

- Tier 1: The organization's top levels of management, policies for the organization, and the procedural metrics results for overall risk management.
- Tier 2: Encompasses the business processes and their interaction with tiers 1 and 3, application of risk management strategies.
- Tier 3: Focus is on the hardware, software, and technical procedures involvement with the continuous monitoring program. Provides metrics to all upward-level tiers on the effectiveness of the continuous monitoring program.

Continuous monitoring is part of the organization's overall risk management process and is the effect of good practices, discipline, and a well-trained staff. NIST identifies tier involvement as

Tier 1—Organization: Risk management activities address high-level information security governance policy as it relates to risk to the organization as a whole, to its core missions, and to its business functions. At this tier, the criteria for continuous monitoring are defined by the organization's risk management strategy, including how the organization plans to assess, respond to, and monitor risk, and the oversight required to ensure that the risk management strategy is effective. Security controls, security status, and other metrics defined and monitored by officials at this tier are designed to deliver information necessary to make risk management decisions in support of governance. Tier 1 metrics are developed for supporting governance decisions regarding the organization, its core missions, and its business functions. Tier 1 metrics may be calculated based on security-related information from common, hybrid, and system-specific security controls. The metrics and the frequency with which they are monitored and reported are determined by requirements to maintain operations within organizational risk tolerances. As part of the overall governance structure established by the organization, the tier 1 risk management strategy and the associated monitoring requirements are communicated throughout tiers 2 and 3.

Tier 2—Mission/business processes: Officials that are accountable for one or more missions or business processes (portfolios) are also responsible for overseeing the associated risk management activities for those processes. The tier 2 criteria for continuous monitoring of information security are defined by how core mission/business processes are prioritized with respect to the overall goals and objectives of the organization, the types of information needed to successfully execute the stated mission/business processes, and the organization-wide information security program strategy. Controls in the program management (PM) (NIST

SP 800-53A) family are an example of tier 2 security controls. These controls address the establishment and management of the organization's information security program. Tier 2 controls are deployed organization-wide and support all information systems. They may be tracked at tier 2 or tier 1. The frequencies with which tier 2 security controls are assessed and security status and other metrics are monitored are determined in part by the objectives and priorities of the mission or business process and measurement capabilities inherent in the infrastructure. Security-related information may come from common, hybrid, and system-specific controls. Metrics and dashboards can be useful at tiers 1 and 2 in assessing, normalizing, communicating, and correlating monitoring activities below the mission/business processes tier in a meaningful manner.

Tier 3—Information systems: Activity at tier 3 addresses risk management from an information system viewpoint. These activities include ensuring that all system-level security controls (technical, operational, and management controls) are implemented correctly, operate as intended, produce the desired outcome with respect to meeting the security requirements for the system, and continue to be effective over time. Continuous monitoring activities at tier 3 also include assessing and monitoring hybrid and common controls implemented at the system level. Security status reporting at this tier often includes but is not limited to security alerts, security incidents, and identified threat activities, including incident response reporting metrics. Continuous monitoring strategy for tier 3 also ensures that security-related information supports the monitoring requirements of other organizational tiers so each tier corresponds to the others in its mitigation and monitoring response. Data feeds/assessment results from system-level controls (system specific, hybrid, or common), along with associated security status reporting, support risk-based decisions at the organization and mission/business processes tiers. System-specific, hybrid, and common controls are defined within the policy of the organization:

- *System specific* identifies controls that are directed at the information system or application(s) and what measures are required for that system security level.
- *Hybrid controls* are a combination of controls from the common set and system specific that are applied as a single control for the system or applications(s). A hybrid control can also be a control that has been modified to address your specific information system's security.
- *Common controls* are generic controls, often referred to as corporate, general, or organizational controls, that are applied across the infrastructure and are normally part of the overall system security posture. A common control could be an authentication software package that meets the criteria for login and is housed within a network support server and supports all platforms.

Information is tailored for each tier and delivered in ways that inform risk-based decision making at all tiers. Those resulting decisions impact the continuous monitoring strategy applied at the information systems tier. Continuous monitoring metrics originating at the information systems tier can be used to assess, respond, analyze trends, and monitor risk across the organization. The ongoing monitoring activities implemented at the information systems tier provide security-related information to stakeholders in support of ongoing system authorization decisions and to the risk executive (function) in support of ongoing organizational risk management.

When developing your process and procedures and aligning them with the business model, the continuous monitoring strategy, implementing the program, and including activities at the organization, mission/business process, and information systems tiers will be a methodical growth process that should not be rushed. Way too many times I have seen these type of ad hoc programs fail and become a critical issue in the continued overall health of the business. So, a well-designed continuous monitoring strategy encompasses security controls assessment, security status monitoring, and security status reporting in support of timely risk-based decision making throughout the organization. It also incorporates processes to ensure that correct response actions are taken. An organization's strategy for based on the data collected is as important (if not more important) than collecting the data. The process for developing a continuous monitoring strategy and implementing a continuous monitoring program is as follows:

- Establish a continuous monitoring program determining metrics, status monitoring frequencies, and control assessment frequencies, and a continuous monitoring technical architecture.
- Define a continuous monitoring strategy based on risk tolerance that maintains clear visibility into assets, awareness of vulnerabilities, up-to-date threat information, and mission/business impacts.
- Implement a continuous monitoring program and collect the security-related information required for metrics, assessments, and reporting. Automate collection, analysis, and reporting of data where possible.
- Analyze the data collected and report findings, determining the appropriate response. It may be necessary to collect additional information to clarify or supplement existing monitoring data.
- Respond to findings with technical, management, and operational mitigating activities or acceptance, transference/sharing, or avoidance/rejection.
- Review and update the monitoring program, adjusting the continuous monitoring strategy and maturing measurement capabilities to increase visibility into assets and awareness of vulnerabilities, further enable data-driven control of the security of an organization's information infrastructure, and increase organizational resilience.

The organizational security architecture, operational security capabilities, and monitoring processes will improve and mature over time to better respond to the dynamic threat and vulnerability landscape. An organization's continuous monitoring strategy and program are routinely reviewed for relevance and are revised as needed to increase visibility into assets and awareness of vulnerabilities and to use the proper mitigation steps for each threat or vulnerability encountered. This further enables data-driven control of the security of an organization's information infrastructure, and increases organizational flexibility when determining the path to meet its security needs/requirements. Additionally, this aids in the organization's ability to provide a secure, cost-effective computing base.

A business's monitoring practices cannot be efficiently achieved through manual or automated processes alone. Monitoring is more than a simple Intrusion Detection System (IDS), firewall, or gateway. Effective continuous monitoring also involves the policies, procedures, and physical security checks used within the infrastructure. Where manual processes are used, the processes are repeatable and verifiable to enable consistent implementation. Automated processes, including the use of automated support tools (e.g., vulnerability scanning tools, network scanning devices, log consolidation), can make the process of continuous monitoring more cost-effective, consistent, and efficient. Many of the technical security controls defined in NIST SP 800–53, *Recommended Security Controls for Federal Information Systems and Organizations*, are good candidates for monitoring using automated tools and techniques. Real-time monitoring of implemented technical controls using automated tools can provide an organization with a much more dynamic view of the effectiveness of those controls, their ability to respond, and the security posture of the organization. It is important to recognize that with any comprehensive information security program, all implemented security controls, including management and operational controls, must be regularly assessed for effectiveness, even if the monitoring of such controls cannot be automated or is not easily automated.

Organizations should take the following steps to establish, implement, and maintain an effective continuous monitoring practice:

- Establish a continuous monitoring program.
- Define a continuous monitoring strategy.
- Implement a continuous monitoring program.
- Analyze data and report findings (trend analysis).
- Respond to findings.
- Review and update the continuous monitoring strategy and program.

A robust continuous monitoring program enables organizations to move from compliance-driven risk management to a more data-driven risk management program, providing organizations with information necessary to support risk response decisions, security status information, and ongoing insight into security control effectiveness.

Continuous Monitoring Strategy

Effective continuous monitoring begins with development of a strategy that addresses continuous monitoring requirements and activities at each organizational tier (organization, mission/business processes, and information systems). Each tier monitors security metrics and assesses security control effectiveness with established monitoring and assessment frequencies and status reports customized to support tier-specific decision making. Policies, procedures, tools, and templates that are implemented from tiers 1 and 2, or that are managed in accordance with guidance from tiers 1 and 2, best support shared use of data within and across tiers. The lower tiers may require information in addition to that required at higher tiers, and hence develop tier-specific strategies that are consistent with those at higher tiers and still sufficient to address local tier requirements for decision making. Depending on the organization, there may be overlap in the tasks and activities conducted at each tier; this overlap helps in a contiguous program.

The following guidelines, though not doctrinaire, help to ensure an organization-wide approach to continuous monitoring that best stimulates standardized methodologies and reliable practices, and hence maximizes efficiencies and leveragability of security-related data. As changes occur, the continuous monitoring strategy is reviewed for relevance, accuracy in reflecting organizational risk tolerances, correctness of measurements, and applicability of metrics. An inherent part of any continuous monitoring strategy is the inclusion of criteria describing the conditions that trigger a review or update of the strategy, in addition to the defined frequency audit. Likewise, the organization defines criteria and procedures for updating the continuous monitoring program based on the revised continuous monitoring strategy.

Organization (Tier 1) and Mission/Business Processes (Tier 2)

The risk executive (function) determines the overall organizational risk tolerance and risk mitigation strategy at the organization tier.

When developed at tiers 1 and 2, the following policies, procedures, and templates facilitate organization-wide, standardized processes in support of the continuous monitoring strategy. The continuous monitoring strategy is developed and implemented to support risk management in accordance with the risk tolerance level of the organization. While continuous monitoring strategy, policy, and procedures may be developed at any tier, typically, the organization-wide continuous monitoring strategy and associated policy are developed at the organization tier with general procedures for implementation developed at the mission/business processes tier. If the organization-wide strategy is developed at the mission/business processes tier, tier 1 officials review and approve the strategy to ensure that organizational risk tolerance across all missions and business processes has been appropriately considered. This information is communicated to staff at the mission/business processes and information systems tiers and reflected in mission/business processes and information systems tier strategy, policy, and procedures.

- Policy that defines key metrics
- Policy for modifications to and maintenance of the monitoring strategy
- Policy and procedures for the assessment of security control effectiveness (common, hybrid, and system-level controls)
- Policy and procedures for security status monitoring
- Policy and procedures for security status reporting (on control effectiveness and status monitoring)
- Policy and procedures for assessing risks and gaining threat information and insights
- Policy and procedures for configuration management and security impact analysis
- Policy and procedures for implementation and use of organization-wide tools
- Policy and procedures for establishment of monitoring frequencies
- Policy and procedures for determining sample sizes and populations and for managing object sampling
- Procedures for determining security metrics and data sources
- Templates for assessing risks

- Templates for security status reporting (on control effectiveness and status monitoring)

Policy, procedures, and templates necessarily address manual and automated monitoring methodologies. Additionally at these tiers, organizations establish policy and procedures for training of personnel with continuous monitoring roles. This may include training on management and use of automated tools (e.g., establishing baselines and tuning of measurements to provide accurate monitoring of operational environments). It may also include training for recognition of and appropriate response to triggers and alerts from metrics indicating risks beyond acceptable limits, as well as training on internal or external reporting requirements. This training may be included in existing role-based training requirements for those with significant security roles, or it may consist of training specifically focused on implementation of the organization's continuous monitoring policy and procedures.

When implementing policies, procedures, and templates developed at higher tiers, lower tiers fill in any gaps related to their tier-specific processes. Decisions and activities by tier 1 and 2 officials may be constrained by things such as mission/business needs, limitations of the infrastructure (including the human components), immutable governance policies, and external drivers.

Information System (Tier 3)

The system-level continuous monitoring strategy is developed and implemented to support risk management, not only at the information systems tier, but at all three tiers in accordance with system and organizational risk tolerance. Although the strategy may be defined at tier 1 or 2, system-specific policy and procedures for implementation may also be developed at tier 3. System-level security-related information includes assessment data pertaining to system-level security controls and metrics data obtained from system-level security controls. System owners establish a system-level strategy for continuous monitoring by considering factors such as the system's architecture and operational environment, manning structure, and organizational and mission-level requirements, System-level continuous monitoring addresses monitoring security controls for effectiveness (assessments), monitoring for security status, and reporting findings. At a minimum, all security controls, including common and hybrid controls implemented at the system level, are assessed for policy, procedures, and templates.

The continuous monitoring strategy is designed, in part, to help ensure that compromises to the security architecture are managed in a way to prevent or minimize impact on business and mission functions.

Stakeholders, management, operations, and technical representatives should all take part in determining assessment frequencies of security controls based on drivers from all three tiers. A full discussion of factors to consider when determining assessment and monitoring frequencies is included in the "Monitoring and Assessment Frequencies" section of this chapter.

The continuous monitoring strategy at the information systems tier also supports ongoing authorization. Ongoing authorization implies recurring updates to the authorization decision information in accordance with assessment and monitoring frequencies. Assessment results from monitoring common controls implemented and managed at the organization or mission/business process tier may be combined with information generated at the information systems tier in order to provide the stakeholders with a complete set of independently generated evidence.

Process Roles and Responsibilities

Tiers 1 and 2 officials have responsibilities throughout the continuous monitoring process, including, but not limited to, the following: provide input to the development of the organizational continuous monitoring strategy, including establishment of metrics, policy, and procedures; compiling and correlating tier 3 data into security-related information of use at tiers 1 and 2; establishment of policies on assessment and monitoring frequencies; and provisions for ensuring sufficient depth and coverage when sampling methodologies are utilized.

Technical representatives need only be independent of the operation of the system. They may be from within the organizational tier, the mission/business tier, or some other independent entity, internal or external to the organization. Results of assessments done by system operators can be used if they have been validated by independent technical representatives. This system information is an outcome of the risk management process. Electronic standardized templates and document management systems (portals) readily support frequent updates with data generated by continuous monitoring programs.

- Review monitoring results (security-related information) to determine security status in accordance with organizational policy and definitions of continuous monitoring.
- Analyze potential security impact to organization and mission/business process functions resulting from changes to information systems and their environments of operation, along with the security impact to the enterprise architecture resulting from the addition or removal of information systems.
- Make a determination as to whether or not current risk is within organizational risk tolerance levels.
- Take steps to respond to risk as needed (e.g., request new or revised metrics, additional or revised assessments, modifications to existing common security controls, or additional controls) based on the results of ongoing monitoring activities and assessment of risk.
- Update relevant security documentation.
- Review new or modified legislation, directives, policies, etc., for any changes to security requirements.
- Review monitoring results to determine if organizational plans and policies should be adjusted or updated.
- Review monitoring results to identify new information on vulnerabilities.
- Review information on new or emerging threats as evidenced by threat activities present in monitoring results, threat modeling (asset and attack based), industry security reports, and other information available through trusted sources.

Tier 3 officials have responsibilities throughout the continuous monitoring process, including, but not limited to, the following:

- Provide input to the development and implementation of the organization-wide continuous monitoring strategy along with development and implementation of the system-level continuous monitoring.

- Support planning and implementation of security controls, the deployment of automation tools, and how those tools interface with one another in support of the continuous monitoring.
- Determine the security impact of changes to the information system and its environment of operation, including changes associated with commissioning or decommissioning the system.
- Assess ongoing security control effectiveness.
- Take steps to respond to risk as needed (e.g., request additional or revised assessments, modify existing security controls, implement additional security controls, accept risk, etc.) based on the results of ongoing monitoring activities, assessment of risk, and outstanding items in the plan of action and milestones.
- Provide ongoing input to the security plan, security assessment report, and plan of action and milestones based on the results of the continuous monitoring process.
- Report the security status of the information system, including the data needed to inform tiers 1 and 2 metrics.
- Review the reported security status of the information system to determine whether the risk to the system and the organization remains within organizational risk tolerances.

Define Sample Populations

You may find that collecting data from every object of every system within an organization may be impractical or cost-prohibitive. Sampling is a methodology employable with both manual and automated monitoring that may make continuous monitoring more cost-effective. A risk with sampling is that the sample population may fail to capture the variations in assessment outcomes that would be obtained from an assessment of the full population. This could result in an inaccurate view of security control effectiveness and organizational security status.

NIST SP 800-53A describes how to achieve satisfactory coverage when determining sample populations for the three named assessment methods: examine, interview, and test. The guidelines in NIST SP 800-53A are for basic, focused, and comprehensive testing and help to address the general issue of sampling, particularly that of coverage. In selecting a sample population, the coverage attribute is satisfied through consideration of three criteria (listed below): addresses the need for a "representative sample of assessment objects" or a "sufficiently large sample of assessment objects." Statistical tools can be used to help quantify sample size.

Types of objects: Ensure sufficient diversity of types of assessment objects.

Number of each type: Choose enough objects of each type to provide confidence that assessment of additional objects will result in consistent findings.

Specific objects per type assessed: Given all of the objects of relevance throughout the organization that could be assessed, include enough objects per type in the sample population to sufficiently account for the known or anticipated variance in assessment outcomes.

Prior to initial authorization, the system is not included in the organization's continuous monitoring program.

The *NIST Engineering Statistics Handbook* describes that when deciding how many objects to include in sample populations, the following should be considered:

- Desired information (What question will the measurements help answer?)
- Cost and practicality of making the assessment
- Information already known about the objects, organization, or operating environments
- Anticipated variability across the total population
- Desired confidence in resulting statistics and conclusions drawn about the total population

Ways to achieve "increased" or "further increased grounds for confidence that a control is implemented correctly and operating as intended" across the entire organization include asking more targeted questions, increasing the types of objects assessed, and increasing the number of each type of object assessed.

Organizations may also target specific objects for assessment in addition to the random sample, using the above criteria. However, sampling methods other than random sampling are used with care to avoid introducing bias. Automated data collection and analysis can reduce the need for sampling.

Continuous Monitoring Program

Organizations establish a program to implement the continuous monitoring strategy. The program is sufficient to inform risk-based decisions and maintain operations within established risk tolerances. Goals include detection of anomalies and changes in the organization's environments of operation and information systems, visibility into assets, awareness of vulnerabilities, knowledge of threats, security control effectiveness, and security status, including compliance. Metrics are designed and frequencies determined to ensure that information needed to manage risk to within organizational risk tolerances is available. Tools, technologies, and manual or automated methodologies are implemented within the context of an architecture designed to deliver the required information in the appropriate context and at the right frequencies.

Determine Metrics

Organizations determine metrics to be used to evaluate and control ongoing risk to the organization. Metrics, which include all the security-related information from assessments and monitoring produced by automated tools and manual procedures, are organized into meaningful information to support decision making and reporting requirements. Metrics should be derived from specific objectives that will maintain or improve security posture. Metrics are developed for system-level data to make them meaningful in the context of mission/ business or organizational risk management.

Metrics may use security-related information acquired at different frequencies, and therefore with varying data latencies. Metrics may be calculated from a combination of security status monitoring, security control assessment data, and data collected from one or more security controls. Metrics may be determined at any tier or across an organization. Some examples of metrics are the number and severity of vulnerabilities revealed and remediated, number of unauthorized access attempts, configuration baseline information, contingency plan testing dates and results, and number of employees who are current on awareness training requirements, risk tolerance thresholds for organizations, and the risk score associated with a given system configuration.

As an example, a metric that an organization might use to monitor the status of authorized and unauthorized components on a network could rely on related metrics such as physical asset locations, logical asset locations (subnets/Internet Protocol (IP) addresses), media access control (MAC) addresses, system association, and policies/procedures for network connectivity. The metrics would be refreshed at various frequencies in accordance with the continuous monitoring strategy. The metrics might be computed hourly, daily, or weekly. Though logical asset information might change daily, it is likely that policies and procedures for network connectivity will be reviewed or revised no more than annually. These metrics are informative only and are not recommended metrics. They are included to assist in explaining the concept of metrics as they are applied across tiers. Organizations define their own metrics and associated monitoring frequencies. In order to calculate metrics, associated controls and their objects are assessed and monitored with frequencies consistent with the timing requirements expressed in the metric.

It should be noted that metrics are fundamentally flawed without assurance that all security controls are implemented correctly. Metrics are defined or calculated in accordance with output from the security architecture. Collecting metrics from security architecture with security controls that have not been assessed is equivalent to using a broken or uncalibrated scale. The interpretation of metrics data presumes that controls directly and indirectly used in the metric calculation are implemented and working as anticipated. If a metric indicates a problem, the root cause could be any number of things. Without fundamental assurance of correct implementation and continued effectiveness of security controls that are not associated with the metric, the root cause analysis is going to be hampered, and the analysis may be inappropriately narrowed to a predetermined list, overlooking the true problem.

Monitoring and Assessment Frequencies

Determining frequencies for security status monitoring and security control assessments is a critical function of the organization's continuous monitoring program. For some organizations, dashboards and ongoing assessments are a shift away from the model of complete security control assessments conducted at a distinct point in time. For this shift to be constructive and effective from security assurance and resource use perspectives, organizations determine the frequencies with which each security control or control element is assessed for effectiveness and the frequencies with which each metric is monitored.

Security control effectiveness across a tier or throughout the organization can itself be taken as a security metric, and as such may have an associated status monitoring frequency. Though monitoring and assessment frequencies are determined for each individual metric and control, organizations use these data of different latencies to create a holistic view of the security of each system as well as a view of the security of the enterprise architecture. As the monitoring program matures, monitoring and assessment frequencies are important in the context of how the data are used, and the question "When did the system receive authorization to operate?" will become less meaningful than "How resilient is the system?"

Considerations in Determining Assessment and Monitoring Frequencies

Organizations should take the following criteria into consideration when establishing monitoring frequencies for metrics or assessment frequencies for security controls.

As an example, the below project plan is provided:

Phase 1: Project Initiation/Development

   Scope: Generally the scope comes from the proposal request and the client defines what it is it wants you to do and for what reason. You should not copy this verbatim; understand it and write to it—write to what the client wants and what the "boundaries" of your analysis will extend. Be careful and make sure that the scope is clear, concise, and what the client wants. For example, the BIA defines the requirements of the financial division of the XYZ Company and encompasses the established boundaries of system A, B, C.... As part of the analysis we will....

Objectives and deliverables: State the objective and what deliverables you intend to provide for the client. Your objectives should match those of the requirements statement or the request for quote (RFQ). Give them what they want, not what you think they want. Sometimes it is hard to write literally—teamwork makes it happen.

Method of collection: How do you intend to collect the data that are going to be considered "evidence" that will back up your claims delivered at the presentation? Make sure the numbers add up. There is nothing worse than having a client correct you while you are presenting your claims and solution; it destroys your credibility.

- Identify people
- Interview order

Phase 2: Discovery and Collection

- General information
- Process information
- Dependencies and interconnections

Interconnections are a very important part of the overall business model and are highly misunderstood and unfortunately an ignored process. An information system or application connecting to another information system application to perform a requested function is an interconnection and needs to be identified and secured (i.e., you log into a web-based application and request your bank balance for review and transfer of funds from one account, checking, to another account, savings). You have multiple events taking place and are not logging into the bank server that actually holds your account data, but merely a front-end application that retrieves the data from some form of a database system. In the infrastructure portion of this, how is that interconnection identified? What role does it play in the business model? How secure is the interconnection of each system? In the federal sector the security officers develop a document that is referred to as the trusted facility manual (TFM). The TFM is documentation that includes guide(s) or manual(s) for the system's privileged users. The manual(s) provide information on

1. Configuring, installing, and operating the system
2. Making optimum use of the system's security features
3. Identifying known security vulnerabilities regarding the configuration and use of administrative functions

Something that is overlooked is the process of updating the document(s) as new vulnerabilities are identified. As most documented processes, they get left behind. A document management system should be incorporated with a minimum of semiannual reviews.

- Required resources
- Potential impact

Phase 3: Application and Data Criticality

- Application information
- Database information
- Hardware information
- Network information

Phase 4: Analyze the Data

- Review business unit BIA
- Follow-up meetings
- Report the results
- Final report and presentation
- Creation of executive report
- Presentations

Next Steps

What do you think should come next?

11

PHYSICAL SECURITY

Physical security, its requirements, and implementation process are all individual steps to becoming and providing a more secure environment to work. Throughout the next few pages I hope to present to you a methodical way to implement the physical aspects of developing a secure infrastructure. This goes beyond the "gates, guns, and guards" (G³). Although G³ are the basics, let's look at each aspect of designing a secure environment, examine each event, and understand how each event adds to the overall posture of your infrastructure. When we look at physical security, I like to take the approach in design from the outside in and then backwards. This helps me ensure that I have covered all aspects of the facilities and possibilities of error (Figure 11.1).

Defense in depth applies to more than just your information technology aspects of security. In physical security it is somewhat difficult to establish metrics for a total view and then apply the performance measurements and testing that are necessary for effective management and oversight. The process of testing can become burdensome if senior management does not utilize the tests properly. The operational and management scope of physical security can face obstacles in developing meaningful, outcome-oriented performance goals and in collecting data that can be used to assess the true impact of building protection efforts. Without consistent management support, performance measurement and testing have the potential to become counterproductive and could evolve into ends in themselves, rather than serving as a means of ensuring program success. So when developing your metrics you need to keep this in mind and try to develop goals that are straightforward and realistic. This we will attempt to develop in this chapter. Overcoming these obstacles will require sustained leadership, long-term investment, and clearly defined performance goals and data.

The costs associated with developing the initial requirements, particularly to establish performance databases, will require significant

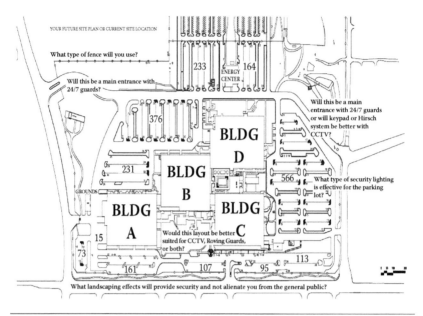

Figure 11.1   Your current or future location.

front-end funding. At the agency level, leadership must communicate the mission-related priority and commitment assigned to performance measurement actions. Management attention will be required at the building level as well to ensure buy-in and cooperation among building operators, security managers, building occupants, and other stakeholders. If management can meet these challenges, the physical security performance measures will help to ensure accountability, prioritize security needs, and justify investment decisions to maximize available resources.

History

Over the past few decades the United States has been targeted by multiple groups with malicious intent, from internal and external sources. Each event was designed to make a point about something. Some say the following events changed the way Americans live; others still walk around like sheep. Here are the most significant events:

- September 11, 2001: Terrorists hijack four U.S. commercial airliners taking off from various locations on the East Coast of the United States in a coordinated suicide attack.

In separate attacks, two of the airliners crash into the Twin Towers of the World Trade Center in New York City, which catch fire and eventually collapse. A third airliner crashes into the Pentagon in Washington, D.C., causing extensive damage. The fourth airliner, also believed to be heading toward Washington, D.C., crashes outside Shanksville, Pennsylvania, killing all 45 people on board. Casualty estimates from New York put the possible death toll close to 5,000, while as many as 200 people may have been lost at the Pentagon crash site.

- October 12, 2000: A terrorist bomb damages the destroyer *USS Cole* in the port of Aden, Yemen, killing 17 sailors and injuring 39.
- August 7, 1998: Terrorist bombs destroy the U.S. embassies in Nairobi, Kenya, and Dar es Salaam, Tanzania. In Nairobi, 12 Americans are among the 291 killed, and over 5,000 are wounded, including 6 Americans. In Dar es Salaam, 1 U.S. citizen is wounded among the 10 killed and 77 injured.
  - In response, on August 20 the United States attacked targets in Afghanistan and Sudan with over 75 cruise missiles ($830,000 each) fired from Navy ships in the Arabian and Red Seas. About 60 Tomahawk cruise missiles were fired from warships in the Arabian Sea. Most struck six separate targets in a camp near Khost, Afghanistan. Simultaneously, about 20 cruise missiles were fired from U.S. ships in the Red Sea, striking a factory in Khartoum, Sudan, which was suspected of producing components for making chemical weapons.
- June 21, 1998: Rocket-propelled grenades explode near the U.S. embassy in Beirut.
- July 27, 1996: A pipe bomb explodes during the Olympic Games in Atlanta, killing 1 person and wounding 111.
- June 25, 1996: A bomb aboard a fuel truck explodes outside a U.S. Air Force installation in Dhahran, Saudi Arabia. Nineteen U.S. military personnel are killed in the Khubar Towers housing building, and 515 are wounded, including 240 Americans.

With each event something happened to the level of awareness about terrorism. Since 1986 there have been over 117 terrorist events within the world. Once again, each event was to express something, and once again, it changed the level of awareness. In America, since April 20, 1995, the day after the bombing of the Murrah Building in Oklahoma City, the president directed the U.S. Department of Justice (DOJ) to assess the vulnerability of federal office facilities to terrorism. In June 1995, the DOJ issued the *Vulnerability Assessment of Federal Facilities* report, establishing new building security standards. The report changed the way we look at facilities and design building security plans. The study also showed where designers were lacking when it came to performing an assessment of the area and assigning the security level of the building. Many new criteria were added that incorporated the business model and assets needed to perform each level of business, from management to the technical performance. Risk is part of everything we do in security. Later we will hopefully show how it can be mitigated to an acceptable level.

Security Level (SL) Determination

The initial SL determination for new leased or owned space will be made as soon as practical after the identification of a space require-ment (including succeeding leases). The determination should be made early enough in the space acquisition process to allow for the implementation of required countermeasures (or reconsideration of the acquisition caused by an inability to meet minimum physical security requirements). The initial risk assessment should be com-pleted and placed on file for reference to maintain continuity between this and future evaluations. The chief security officer (CSO) should ensure that risk assessments are conducted at least every five years for level A and B facilities, at least every three years for level C and D facilities, and every year for level E buildings or campuses. The SL should be reviewed and adjusted, if necessary, as part of each initial and recurring risk assessment. This should be part of the physical security plan and the overall outcome included in annual reporting and planning meetings for the company; an example is provided in Facility Security Level.xlsx, provided in the additional materials on the CRC Press website.

The responsibility for making the final SL determination rests with the CSO after consultation and input with other stakeholders, who must either accept the risk or fund security measures to reduce the risk:

- For single-tenant-owned or -leased facilities, a representative of the major tenant agency will make the SL determination, in consultation with the owning or leasing department or agency and the security organization(s) responsible for the building.
  - Future upgrades and requirements should be part of the lease agreement.
- In multi-tenant-owned or -leased facilities, the corporate liaison in coordination with a representative of each tenant (i.e., the building security committee [BSC]) will make the SL determination, in consultation with the owning or leasing company and the security organization(s) responsible for the building.

When the security organization(s) and the owner/leasing authority do not agree with the tenant agency representative with regard to the SL determination, the building owner/major lessee will facilitate the final determination. The determination should be made through the use of a professionally certified building threat agency.

The SL determination should be documented, signed, and retained by all parties to the decision.

Threat Factors/Criteria

To establish the SL, it is important to consider factors that make the building a target for adversarial acts (threats), as well as those that characterize the value or criticality of the building (consequences). The Physical_Security_Checklist.docx located in the additional materials on the CRC Press website identifies a number of factors to consider in determining a building's security level. However, size and population are not the only two criteria attributable to establishing a security level. The Physical Security Checklist and this chapter identify other factors, including the degree of public contact, the type of activities carried out (mission), and the type of agencies located in the building. The list provides only limited guidance for applying those factors. In many cases, a single building has features that meet criteria of multiple security levels outlined in this chapter, making it difficult to categorize, and best practices needs to become a factor. The Physical Security Checklist and this chapter take into account size and population, as well as several other factors that determine the value of the building to the company and to potential adversaries.

Just as the criteria established are based largely on malicious targeting, the criteria incorporated in this methodology are based upon an analysis of crime (as established by the FBI Crime Statistics: http://www.fbi. gov/stats-services/crimestats) and other factors targeting as it is understood today, and the assessed objectives of activity in your local area:

- What level of crime is in the area and what are the targeted sources? Review local reports and talk to the surrounding businesses for input.
- Terrorists, gangs, and malicious persons seeking to destroy, incapacitate, or exploit critical infrastructure and resources across the enterprise to threaten security, cause mass casualties, weaken your profits, and damage public morale and confidence.
- Corporate or commercial companies should be able to carry out at any point, including during a major disaster. The continuity of these fundamental activities, as well as primary mission-essential functions and other essential functions, is a part of determining the value of a building to the company.
- Finally, the threat to your facilities from criminal elements must also be evaluated in determining the SL. Consideration must be given to the risk from more common criminal acts, such as theft, assault, unlawful demonstrations, workplace violence, and vandalism—acts that historically occur more frequently at corporate or commercial facilities than acts of terrorism.

Building Security Level Matrix

The SL matrix uses four weighted security factors to be evaluated, with corresponding points of 1, 2.5, 3, or 5 allocated for each factor. This provides the criteria to be used in evaluating each factor and assigning points. However, the criteria cannot capture all of the circumstances that could be encountered. Thus, the matrix includes a fifth factor—the plus or minus (±) change—to allow the inspector

Security Level Evaluation Score Sheet					
Points					
Agent	1	2.5	3	5	Total
Mission/business	Low	Moderate	High	Extreme	
Public impact	Low	Moderate	High	Extreme	
Building occupants	<50	51–175	176–800	>800	
Building square footage	<5,000	5,001–15,000	15,001–100,000	>100,000	
Impact on tenants	Low	Moderate	High	Extreme	
					Total
Security level points	I	II	III	IV	Initial SL
	5–9	10–15	16–20	21–25	
Other factors	Adjustment authorization/justification				±2 SL
					Final SL

Figure 11.2   Security level evaluation score sheet.

to consider other factors unique to the company's needs or to the building's overall occupancy.

Additionally, although the requirement for evaluation judgment has been reduced to the extent possible, it may still be necessary. To that end, this document includes an explanation of why each factor was included, a description of its intended impact on the score, and examples to allow security professionals encountering conditions that do not clearly match those anticipated here to make an informed decision based on the same rationale used in the development of this process.

To use the SL matrix, each of the factors will be examined and a point value assigned based on the scoring criteria provided. The points for all factors will then be added together and a preliminary SL identified, based on the sum (Figure 11.2). The inspectors may then consider any changes that may be associated with the building. An adjustment to the SL may be made (and documented) accordingly, and a final SL determined.

Building Security Level Scoring Criteria

Mission/Business

The value of a building to the company is based largely on the mission of the dominant occupant, particularly as it may relate to

Value	Score	Description	Facility
Extreme	5	Houses essential communications equipment necessary for operations	Headquarters and business centers
		Occupied by personnel who are necessary for the company operations	Headquarters and business centers
		Occupied by personnel who are foreign owners and business partners	Headquarters and business centers
		Equipment that is necessary to the operation, financial stability, and sustainment of business operations	Company headquarters facility or secondary facility
		Stores data or backup operations that are essential to the continuity of the company	Data primary or backup facility
High	3	Master documents that are essential to the business operations and management oversight	Headquarters and business centers' archival storage
		Business continuity or disaster recovery facility	Data primary or backup facility
Moderate	2.5	Business center or external offices of the company	Secondary facility for sales and limited operations
Low	1	Subcontractor facility that houses personnel and equipment not essential to operations	Off-site facility for limited operations, storage of equipment, or secondary communications outlet

Figure 11.3 Mission criticality.

the mission-essential functions (MEFs) and other important business of the company. As vital as it is for the company to perform these activities, it is equally attractive to adversaries to disrupt important company functions. The mission criticality score is based on the criticality of the missions carried out by tenants in the building (Figure 11.3). In a multitenant or mixed-multitenant building, the highest rating for any tenant in the building should be used for this factor. Business continuity plan (BCP) and continuity of operations (COOP) documents are good sources of information regarding the performance of essential functions.

Public Impact

The representation of the building is based on both its attractiveness as a target (symbolic to plight of aggressor) and the consequences of an event. The public impact value is based on external appearances or well-known/publicized operations within the building that indicate it is a U.S. company building (in a foreign country) or a major player in the country's overall industrial growth. Transnational aggressors often seek to strike at symbols of the United States, democracy, and capitalism; domestic radicals may seek to make a statement against company control, taxation, or regulation, or foreign export or jobs, or imports from other countries.

Public impact is also important because of the potential negative psychological influence of an undesirable event occurring at a prominent corporate or commercial building. Attacks at certain company facilities, particularly those that are perceived to be well protected and central to the safety and well-being of the country, could result in a loss of confidence in the company domestically or internationally, as applicable.

It is also necessary to recognize that even if there are no external appearances or well-known operations of the company, a mixed-tenant or mixed-multitenant building may be symbolic to aggressors with other motivations. For example, facilities such as financial institutions, communications centers, transportation hubs, and controversial testing laboratories may be symbolic in the eyes of single-interest radicals and aggressor organizations, whose leaders have stated that strikes against the company are a high priority. The symbolism of corporate or commercial facilities or a university campus should be assessed similarly (Figure 11.4).

Building Occupants

The intent of most aggressors is the cause and impact of mass casualties and is an acknowledged goal of many aggressor organizations. From a significance standpoint, the potential for mass casualties should be a major consideration and the building population factor should be based on the peak total number of personnel in the area, including employees, on-site contract employees, and visitors.

Value	Score	Description	Facility
Extreme	5	Large corporate facility complex that houses the majority of the corporate infrastructure, a university, or other large facility that will cause public outcry	Corporate complex, university, or data backup facility
		A historical facility for the nation	Museum, corporate archives
		A religious facility, including a church of a specific religion	Central meeting place for prayer, celebration, or schooling
High	3	Corporate headquarters, prominent building within a city	Tall buildings
		Local government facility	Police, fire, emergency response center
Moderate	2.5	Facility of gathering for specific or symbolic might	Sports arena
		Corporate or government-sponsored care facility	Child care, elderly care facility
		Tourist gathering	Historical sites
Low	1	One of many public facilities that may sponsor an event	Local schools, auditorium
		Frequent meeting place for local people	City park, lake

Figure 11.4   Public impact.

The number should not include transient populations, such as an occasional conference (or similar event), unless the building is intended for use in such a manner (such as an auditorium) and the population is part of normal business. Transient shifts in population, such as the occasional conference, should be addressed by situational security measures.

The number of daily visitors should be determined using the best metrics available to ensure the most accurate population. Ideally, this would be achieved through a review of visitor logs or access control lists; however, it may necessitate an estimate or a short-term sampling of visitor throughput.

The public impact of adult and child care centers or buildings with a care center should receive a building population score of moderate and a score of 2.5. If the corporate or commercial population of a single, mixed-tenant, or mixed-multitenant building contributes to the target attractiveness and includes an adult or child care center (e.g., creates a substantial population over and above the corporate or commercial population), document the rationale and add 0.5 point, not to exceed the maximum of 3 points (Figure 11.5).

Building Square Footage

The building size factor is based on all corporate or commercially occupied space in the building, including cases where a company with real property authority controls some other amount of space in the building. If the entire building or all the floors are occupied, gross square footage should be used (length × width); if only portions of floors are occupied in a multitenant building, assignable or rentable square footage should be used (Figure 11.6).

Size may be directly or indirectly proportional to the building population. An office building with a large population will generally have a correspondingly large amount of floor space; however, a large warehouse may have a very small population.

For an aggressor, an attack on an occupied large corporate center with recognizable buildings results in more extensive coverage. However, it should also be understood that large facilities require a more substantial attack to create catastrophic damage, entailing more planning and preparation by adversaries, which could be a deterrent.

Impact	Score	Description
Extreme	5	Greater than 800 occupants
High	3	176–800 occupants
		Corporate-sponsored adult or child care facility
Moderate	2.5	51–175 occupants
		Stand-alone care facility
Low	1	Less than 50 occupants

Figure 11.5 Building occupants.

	Population			
Building square footage	<5,000	5,001–15,000	15,001–100,000	>100,000

Figure 11.6 Building square footage.

From a consequence perspective, the cost to replace or repair a large building is a major consideration. If the total size of a mixed-tenant or mixed-multitenant building beyond that occupied by the corporate or commercial population contributes to the target attractiveness (e.g., creates a highly recognizable structure based on size alone), document the rationale and add 2 points, not to exceed the maximum of 5 points.

Impact on Tenants

Unlike the criticality of the corporate mission/business-essential functions, which should be considered in terms of impact, the impact to tenant agencies score is considered from a perspective of target attractiveness. The building should be viewed in terms of whether the nature of public contact required in or resulting from the conduct of business is adversarial, or whether there is a history of oppositional acts committed at the building, against building tenants, or against the tenant agencies elsewhere.

The highest score applicable to any tenant in a multitenant building should be considered when determining the SL, even though it may be possible to limit the emplacement of countermeasures for that threat to a specific tenant's space or part of the building.

As with the impact of commercial tenants on the building's impact score, the potential threat to corporate or commercial tenants in a mixed-tenant or mixed-multitenant building could result in a collateral risk to corporate or commercial tenants and visitors. Thus, in considering the impact, the threat to all tenants in a building, including visitors, should be considered and the highest score used for the rating (Figure 11.7).

Other Factors

It is not possible for this chapter to take into account all the conditions that may affect the SL decision for all the different corporate or commercial organizations. Certain factors, such as a short duration of occupancy, may reduce the value of the building in terms of impact, which could justify a reduction of the SL. Many factors reflect a reduced value of the building itself, and a corresponding reduction in the impact of its loss should be considered.

Impact	Score	Description	Facility
Extreme	5	Tenant mission/business interacts with certain public issues under laws and compliancy	Courts, state environmental offices, parole offices
		Occupied by personnel who are necessary for the company operations	Headquarters and business centers
		Occupied by personnel who are foreign owners and business partners	Headquarters and business centers
		Stores data or backup operations that are essential to the continuity of the company	Data primary or backup facility
High	3	Closed facility that requires positive identification for access and visitor escorts are required	Corporate HQ and state buildings
Moderate	2.5	Low history of aggressor activity, masked tenants, no documented demonstrations	Corporate HQ and state buildings
Low	1	No public interaction, low visitor rates, and no history of aggressor or violent activity	Any facility closed or open to the public that meets the criteria of low in population

Figure 11.7 Impact to tenants.

Other factors may suggest an increase in the SL, such as the potential for cascading effects or downstream impacts on related situations, or costs associated with the reconstitution of the building.

Experience in building security principles, the country's position economically, and aggressor awareness will impact the SL, and in turn may be raised or lowered one level at the discretion of the deciding authority based on the "other" factors. However, the other factor should not be used to raise or lower the SL in response to a particular situation. The SL characterizes the entire building; concerns about specific threats should be addressed with specific countermeasures, even if they are over and above those required as the baseline for a particular security level.

Short-term events could also temporarily affect the factors evaluated here. Unless these events have a history of recurring, they should not affect the SL determination. Instead, contingency plans should be developed to implement temporary measures until the event has passed. For example, a weeklong conference may increase the population of a building substantially during the conference, or a riot in close proximity of the building, but it should not be considered in the SL determination.

Like all risk management decisions, it is important to document these factors and the resulting adjustments made to the SL total score. The decision-making authority should document any factors and the associated adjustment and retain this information as part of the official building security records.

Level E Facilities

While the incorporation of additional factors and a criterion makes this standard more useful to determine the SL for special use and other unique facilities, such as high-security laboratories, hospitals, or unique storage facilities for chemicals, some facilities may still not fit neatly into the criteria defined here. The criticality of the mission or the symbolic nature of the building could be such that it merits a degree of protection above that specified for a SL level D building, even though the other contributing factors, such as population or square footage, might be scored lower.

Campuses, Complexes, and Corporate or Commercial Centers

A campus consists of two or more corporate or commercial facilities located contiguous to one another and sharing some aspects of the environment (e.g., parking, courtyards, vehicle access roads, or gates) or security features (e.g., a perimeter fence, guard force, or on-site central alarm/closed-circuit television monitoring station). It may also be referred to as a complex or corporate or commercial center.

In the case of a campus that houses a single tenant, such as the HP headquarters campus, an overall SL may be established. In multitenant campuses, either all individual facilities in the campus will be assigned an SL in accordance with this standard, or all tenants may agree to determine an overall SL for the entire campus, treating the entire campus as though it were a multitenant building (using the highest rating of any tenant in the building for each factor).

Changes in the Building Security Level

Changes in the environment at the building, particularly when tenants move in or out, could result in changes in the scoring for the various factors. A small change to the population, such as an increase from 50 to 151 employees, could result in the change in security level. The use of multiple factors in making the SL determination somewhat dilutes the effect of any one factor and all but prevents a small change from causing a change in security level. However, the nature of the tenant (i.e., the criticality of the mission or risk associated with the company itself) moving in or out may also affect the SL.

It may be impractical to adjust the SL every time a tenant moves in or out of a multitenant building; instead, the SL will be reviewed at least as part of the regularly recurring risk assessment and adjusted as necessary. Major changes in the nature of the tenants should merit consideration of whether to review and potentially adjust the SL between the regularly scheduled assessments.

The requirement for recurring risk assessments may in some cases make the argument for a corporate or commercial building to install or retain temporary perimeter security measures rather than permanent installations, given that the risk may decrease later, particularly if the building tenant mix is likely to change.

12

BUILDING SECURITY

Building illumination and security levels are important in the protection of information assets and overall security of personnel, property, and the company. In performing many of these evaluations for federal and state agencies, most have a specific requirement to follow. What is offered below is a standard I have used for years and incorporate into the Physical_Security_Checklist.docx located on the CRC Press website. An additional checklist, titled TruckingIndustrySecur ityCheckList.pdf, is also available for that industry. In performing a physical security evaluation of a facility, ensure you have a badge or pass from building management that allows you the access needed or have a familiar face and person for the area—you will be required to perform a 24/7 evaluation to get the full picture of the physical security posture.

The physical security standards and requirements of most companies have a twofold affect, protection of assets of the company (loss prevention) and protection of the employees. Although loss prevention and security of the company assets seem to be the main reason, the safety and security of personnel are a by-product and also part of the procedures.

Protecting critical assets within the infrastructure, including transportation, loading docks, and operations, is essential for security, public health and safety, and economic vitality, from the national to the local level.

Hopefully, within this chapter, I can impart to you some of the best practices to use and how to evaluate the physical aspects of the infrastructure security program.

Illumination

The Lighting Research Center (LRC) is one of the world's leading university research and education organization devoted to lighting and covers a range of technologies to applications and energy use.

There are numerous research studies, and they and can be located on the LRC website.

Lighting is based on an unaided person visual assessment. Illumination can be one of the most inexpensive and best deterrents for the physical security applications. Table 12.1 will give you some basic minimum levels of lighting that should assist you with your lighting requirements within the corporate areas. Illumination is best described as the amount of light delivered from a uniform light source over a square foot of area measured 1 foot from the source, also known as foot-candle (fc) of light or 1 lumen. Lux (lx) is another term used when measuring light, and it equates to a standard unit for luminance that is lumens per square meter (lm/m2): 1 fc = 10.764 lx.

Table 12.1   Lighting Levels

APPLICATION			ILLUMINATED WIDTH, FT (M)		MINIMUM ILLUMINATION	
TYPE	LIGHTING	AREA	INSIDE	OUTSIDE	FOOT-CANDLE (LUX)[a]	LOCATION
Boundary	Glare	Isolated	25 (7.6)	150 (46)	0.2 (2.1)[b]	Outer lighted edge
	Controlled	Semi-isolated	10 (3.0)	70 (21)	0.4 (4.3)	At fence
					0.2 (2.1)	Outer lighted edge
	Controlled	Nonisolated	20–30 (6.1–9.1)	30–40 (9.1–1.2)	0.4 (4.3)	At fence
					0.4 (4.3)	Outer lighted edge
					0.5 (5.4)	Within
Inner area	Area	General	All	—	0.2–0.5[c]	Entire area
		At structures	50 (15)	—	2.1–5.4	Outside from structure
					1 (11)	
Entry point	Controlled	Pedestrian	25 (7.6)	25 (7.6)	2 (21)	Entry pavement and sidewalk
		Vehicular	50 (15)	50 (15)	1 (11)	

[a] Horizontal plane at ground level unless otherwise noted.
[b] Vertical plane, 3 ft (9 m) above grade.
[c] Use higher value for more sensitive areas.

Lighting for CCTV Surveillance

Lighting requirements for CCTV are considerably higher than those required for direct visual surveillance unless you are using high-end infrared or some very expensive lenses with a wide aperture. The entire assessment zone must have an average initial horizontal illumination level of 2 foot-candle (fc = 21.5 lux) at 6 in. (150 mm) above the ground. The uniformity of illumination in the assessment zone must meet the following requirements: (1) the overall ratio of brightest to darkest regions of the assessment zone must not exceed 8 to 1, and (2) the overall ratio of the average brightest to darkest regions of the assessment zone must not exceed 3 to 1.

Several methods are presently used in achieving these illumination levels. These employ high-pressure sodium vapor roadway luminaires spaced to meet both the CCTV and other security illumination requirements. The most common variety of luminaire is the 250 W unit, while some facilities employ a 400 W unit. Some installations have opted for 150 W luminaires with an instant restrike (the time it takes to relight the bulb element) capability.

Building Security Levels

> **Level E:** A building that contains complete business model functions critical to the overarching existence of the company, such as the corporate headquarters with research and development, fiduciary, and other major functions. A level E building should be similar to a level D building in terms of number of employees and square footage. The missions of level E buildings require that tenants secure the site according to the requirements of the main lease holder or building management. This type of building has a main client of greater than 800 personnel and occupies the majority of the square footage *or is the only occupant*. Smaller tenants are unrelated vendors with a low volume of public traffic. Some of the security functions in place must include:
> 1. Controlled access points to the corporate area that include
>   a. Positive identification systems using multiple factors
>   b. X-ray equipment

    c. Secure room/floor access

    d. Man-traps

  2. Guards (armed/unarmed/roving)

    a. Rover vehicles

    b. Verified lighting that meets x lumens/square foot/ emergency lighting

    c. Controlled parking

  3. Closed-caption television (CCTV)

    a. Validated overlap

    b. Low and bright light

    c. Pan, tilt, zoom (PTZ) no more than six split screens per monitor and person

Level D: A building that has 176 to 800 occupants, high volume of public contact, more than 15,001 to 100,000 ft² of space, and tenant agencies that may include high-risk research and development, human resources and financial records, and highly sensitive corporate records.

  1. Controlled access points to the corporate area that include:

    a. Positive identification systems using multiple factors

    b. X-ray equipment

    c. Secure room/floor access

  2. Guards (armed/unarmed/roving)

    a. Rover vehicles

    b. Lighting/emergency lighting

    c. Separate visitor parking

  3. Closed-caption television (CCTV)

    a. Validated overlap

    b. Low and bright light

    c. CCTV no more than 10 split screens per monitor and person

Level C: A building with 51 to 175 employees, moderate/high volume of public contact, up to 15,000 ft² of space, and tenant agencies that may include law enforcement agencies, corporate research, and corporate records and archives.

  1. Limited-control access points:

    a. Baggage checkpoint

    b. Secure room/floor access

2. Guards (armed/unarmed/roving)
   a. Building lighting/emergency lighting
   b. Separate visitor parking
3. Closed-caption television (CCTV)
   a. Critical loading docks, some doorway access
   b. Low and bright light
   c. CCTV no more than 10 split screens per monitor and person

Level B: A building that has less than 51 employees, moderate volume of public contact, 2,500 to 5,000 ft^2 of space, and activities that are routine in nature.
1. Limited-control access points
2. Guards (unarmed)
3. Some closed-caption television (CCTV)
   a. Critical loading docks, some doorway access
   b. CCTV no more than 10 split screens per monitor and person
4. Adequate lighting

Level A: A building that has 10 or fewer employees, low volume of public contact or contact with only a small segment of the population, and 2,500 or less ft^2 of space, such as a small "store front" type of operation.
1. No access control
2. No guards
3. Some closed-caption television (CCTV)
   a. Critical loading docks, some doorway access
   b. CCTV no more than 10 split screens per monitor and person
4. Adequate lighting

Minimum Security Standards

See Table 12.2.

Entry Security

See Table 12.3.

Table 12.2   Perimeter Security

PERIMETER SECURITY	SECURITY LEVEL				
	A	B	C	D	E
PARKING					
Control of parking	N/A	D	M	M	R
Control of adjacent parking	D	D	D	E	E
Avoid leases in which parking cannot be controlled	N/A	D	D	D	D
Leases should provide security control for parking	N/A	D	D	D	D
Post signs and arrange for the towing of unauthorized vehicles	E	E	M	M	R
ID system and procedures for authorized parking (placard, decal, card key, etc.)	N/A	D	M	M	R
Adequate lighting for parking areas	D	D	M	M	R
CLOSED-CIRCUIT TELEVISION (CCTV) MONITORING					
CCTV surveillance cameras with time-lapse video recording	D	E	E	M	R
Post signs advising of 24-hour video surveillance	D	E	E	M	D
LIGHTING					
Lighting with emergency power backup	N/A	M	M	M	R
PHYSICAL BARRIERS					
Extend physical perimeter with concrete or steel barriers	N/A	N/A	D	E	R
Parking barriers	N/A	N/A	D	E	D

Note: R = required, M = minimum standard, E = standard based on building evaluation, D = desirable, N/A = not applicable.

Interior Security

See Table 12.4.

Security Planning

See Table 12.5.

Using the tables provided, practical experience, a developed team, and company familiarity all encompass a thorough evaluation of the requirements and need for the company. Although not inclusive of every business nature, attempt to use the tables as a guide to assist you in developing a safe and security-minded environment for the occupants of the building.

Table 12.3 Entry Security

	SECURITY LEVEL				
ENTRY SECURITY	A	B	C	D	E
RECEIVING/SHIPPING					
Review receiving/shipping procedures (current)	D	M	M	M	R
Implement receiving/shipping procedures (modified)	D	E	M	M	R
ACCESS CONTROL					
Evaluate area for security guard requirements	N/A	E	M	M	R
Security guard patrol	N/A	D	E	E	E
Intrusion detection system with central monitoring capability	N/A	F	M	M	R
Upgrade to current life safety standards (fire detection, fire suppression systems, etc.)	M	M	M	M	D
ENTRANCES/EXITS					
X-ray and magnetometer at public entrances	N/A	D	E	M	R
Require x-ray screening of all mail/packages	N/A	D	E	M	R
Peepholes	F	F	N/A	N/A	N/A
Intercom	F	F	N/A	N/A	N/A
Entry control with CCTV and door strikes	D	F	E	D	R
High-security locks	D	M	M	M	R

Note: R = required, M = minimum standard, E = standard based on building evaluation, D = desirable, N/A = not applicable.

Table 12.4 Interior Security

INTERIOR SECURITY	SECURITY LEVEL				
	A	B	C	D	E
EMPLOYEE/VISITOR IDENTIFICATION					
Agency photo ID for all personnel displayed at all times	N/A	D	E	M	R
Visitor control/screening system	N/A	M	M	M	R
Visitor identification accountability system	N/A	D	E	M	R
Establish ID issuing authority	E	E	E	M	R
UTILITIES					
Prevent unauthorized access to utility areas	E	E	M	M	R
Provide emergency power to critical systems (alarm systems, radio communications, computer facilities, etc.)	D	M	M	M	R
OCCUPANT EMERGENCY PLANS					
Examine occupant emergency plan's (OEP) contingency procedures based on threats	N/A	M	M	M	R
OEP in place, updated annually, periodic testing exercise	N/A	M	M	M	R
Assign and train OEP officials (assignment based on largest tenant in building)	D	M	M	M	R
Annual tenant training	D	M	M	M	R
DAYCARE CENTERS					
Evaluate whether to locate daycare facilities in buildings with high-threat activities	N/A	M	M	M	M
Compare feasibility of locating daycare in facilities outside locations	N/A	M	M	M	M

Note: R = required, M = minimum standard, E = standard based on building evaluation, D = desirable, N/A = not applicable.

Table 12.5 Security Planning

SECURITY PLANNING	SECURITY LEVEL				
	A	B	C	D	E
INTELLIGENCE SHARING					
Establish law enforcement agency/security liaisons	D	M	M	M	R
Review/establish procedure for intelligence receipt and dissemination	D	M	M	M	R
Establish uniform security/threat nomenclature	D	M	M	M	R
TRAINING					
Conduct annual security awareness training	D	M	M	R	R
Establish standardized unarmed guard qualifications/ training requirements	D	M	M	R	R
Establish standardized armed guard qualifications/ training requirements	D	M	M	R	R
TENANT ASSIGNMENT					
Co-locate agencies with similar security needs	N/A	D	D	D	R
Do not co-locate high/low-risk agencies	N/A	D	D	D	R
ADMINISTRATIVE PROCEDURES					
Establish flexible work schedule in high-threat/ high-risk areas to minimize employee vulnerability to criminal activity	D	E	D	D	R
Arrange for employee parking in/near building after normal work hours	D	E	E	M	R
Conduct background security checks and establish security control procedures for service contract personnel	D	M	M	M	R
Establish an account with E-Verify for employee status	D	M	R	R	R
CONSTRUCTION/RENOVATION					
Install Mylar film on all exterior windows (shatter protection)	D	D	E	M	R
Review current projects for blast standards	N/A	M	M	M	R
Review/establish uniform standards for construction	D	M	M	M	R
Review/establish new design standards for blast resistance	E	E	M	M	R
Establish street setback for new construction	D	D	E	M	R

Note: R = required, M = minimum standard, E = standard based on building evaluation, D = desirable, N/A = not applicable.

13

VALIDATING THE ENTERPRISE

Certification and Accreditation Process

The security certification and accreditation (C&A) process consists of four distinct phases

- Initiation phase
- Security certification phase
- Security accreditation phase
- Continuous monitoring phase

Each phase in the security certification and accreditation process consists of a set of well-defined tasks and subtasks that are to be carried out, as indicated, by responsible individuals (e.g., the chief information officer, authorizing official, authorizing official's designated representative, senior agency information security officer, information system owner, information owner, information system security officer, certification agent, and user representatives).

The *initiation phase* consists of three tasks:

1. Preparation
2. Notification and resource identification
3. System security plan review, analysis, and acceptance

The purpose of this phase is to ensure that the authorizing official and senior agency information security officer are in agreement with the contents of the system security plan before the certification agent begins the assessment of the security controls in the information system.

The *security certification phase* consists of two tasks:

1. Security control assessment
2. Security certification documentation

The purpose of this phase is to determine the extent to which the security controls in the information system are implemented correctly, operating as intended, and producing the desired outcome with respect to meeting the security requirements for the system. This phase also addresses specific actions taken or planned to correct deficiencies in the security controls and to reduce or eliminate known vulnerabilities in the information system. Upon successful completion of this phase, the authorizing official will have the information needed from the security certification to determine the risk to agency operations, agency assets, or individuals, and thus will be able to render an appropriate security accreditation decision for the information system.

The *security accreditation phase* consists of two tasks:

1. Security accreditation decision
2. Security accreditation documentation

The purpose of this phase is to determine if the remaining known vulnerabilities in the information system (after the implementation of an agreed upon set of security controls) pose an acceptable level of risk to agency operations, agency assets, or individuals.

Upon successful completion of this phase, the information system owner will have the following:

1. Authorization to operate the information system
2. An interim authorization to operate the information system under specific terms and conditions
3. Denial of authorization to operate the information system

The *continuous monitoring phase* consists of three tasks:

1. Configuration management and control
2. Security control monitoring
3. Status reporting and documentation

The purpose of this phase is to provide oversight and monitoring of the security controls in the information system on an ongoing basis and to inform the authorizing official when changes occur that may impact on the security of the system. The activities in this phase are performed continuously throughout the life cycle of the information system. Figure 13.1 identifies the phase I steps and governing regulations.

Accreditation Decisions

The security *accreditation package* documents the results of the security certification and provides the authorizing official with the

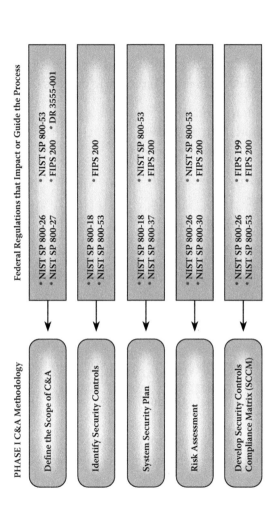

PHASE I C&A Methodology

Federal Regulations that Impact or Guide the Process

Define the Scope of C&A	* NIST SP 800-26 * NIST SP 800-27	* NIST SP 800-53 * FIPS 200 * DR 3555-001
Identify Security Controls	* NIST SP 800-18 * NIST SP 800-53	* FIPS 200
System Security Plan	* NIST SP 800-18 * NIST SP 800-37	* NIST SP 800-53 * FIPS 200
Risk Assessment	* NIST SP 800-26 * NIST SP 800-30	* NIST SP 800-53 * FIPS 200
Develop Security Controls Compliance Matrix (SCCM)	* NIST SP 800-26 * NIST SP 800-53	* FIPS 199 * FIPS 200

Figure 13.1 Phase I methodology and NIST reference.

essential information needed to make a credible, risk-based decision on whether to authorize operation of the information system. Security accreditation decisions resulting from security certification and accreditation processes should be conveyed to information system owners. To ensure the agency's business and operational needs are fully considered, the authorizing official should meet with the information system owner prior to issuing the security accreditation decision to discuss the security certification findings and the terms and conditions of the authorization. There are three types of accreditation decisions that can be rendered by authorizing officials:

- Authorization to operate
- Interim authorization to operate
- Denial of authorization to operate

Examples of security accreditation decision letters appear on the CRC Press website.

Continuous Monitoring

A critical aspect of the security certification and accreditation process is the postaccreditation period involving the continuous monitoring of security controls in the information system over time. An effective continuous monitoring program requires

- Configuration management and configuration control processes
- Security impact analyses on changes to the information system
- Assessment of selected security controls in the information system and security status reporting to appropriate agency officials

Completing a security accreditation ensures that *due diligence* and *due care* have been applied to the decision-making process of an information system, and that it will be operated with appropriate management review, that there is ongoing monitoring of security controls, and that reaccreditation occurs periodically in accordance with federal or agency policy and whenever there is a significant change to the system or its operational environment.

General Process Phase I

The phase I process for identifying security categories (SC), developing the system security plan (SSP), identifying the threats and vulnerabilities within the risk assessment (RA), creating Security Features User Guides (SFUGs), standard operating procedures (SOP), and the configuration management (CM) process is outlined below to assist the client management personnel in identifying with the overall process and assist the C&A team in conducting interviews for the C&A process. Figure 13.2 identifies the security control selection process for evaluating the information systems.

Security Categorization

The C&A process begins by determining the security categorization of the GSSs and MAs. The technical team performs this system categorization by conducting the following tasks: system documentation review and phase I categorization in accordance with NIST SP 800-34 (*Contingency Planning Guide for Information Technology Systems*), NIST 800-60 (*Guide for Mapping Types of Information and Information Systems to Security Categories*), FIPS 199 (*Standards for Security Categorization of Federal Information and Information Systems*), system owner interviews, user interviews, and system administrator interviews (Figure 13.3). These reviews and interviews provide

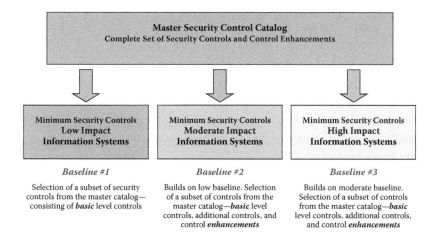

Figure 13.2   Baseline security controls.

FIPS Publication 199	Low	Moderate	High
Confidentiality	The loss of confidentiality could be expected to have a *limited* adverse effect on organizational operations, organizational assets, or individuals.	The loss of confidentiality could be expected to have a *serious* adverse effect on organizational operations, organizational assets, or individuals.	The loss of confidentiality could be expected to have a *severe or catastrophic* adverse effect on organizational operations, organizational assets, or individuals.
Integrity	The loss of integrity could be expected to have a *limited* adverse effect on organizational operations, organizational assets, or individuals.	The loss of integrity could be expected to have a *serious* adverse effect on organizational operations, organizational assets, or individuals.	The loss of integrity could be expected to have a *severe or catastrophic* adverse effect on organizational operations, organizational assets, or individuals.
Availability	The loss of availability could be expected to have a *limited* adverse effect on organizational operations, organizational assets, or individuals.	The loss of availability could be expected to have a *serious* adverse effect on organizational operations, organizational assets, or individuals.	The loss of availability could be expected to have a *severe or catastrophic* adverse effect on organizational operations, organizational assets, or individuals.

Figure 13.3 *Guidance for Mapping Types of Information and Information Systems to FIPS 199 Security Categories.* (From NIST 800-60, http://csrc.nist.gov.)

the information needed to evaluate the confidentiality, integrity, and availability (CIA) of the system that covers 17 security-related areas and its data as established in FIPS 199 and 200 for nonnational defense-related systems, inclusive of NIST 800-53 (*Recommended Security Controls for Federal Information Systems*). The 17 areas represent a broad-based, balanced information security program that addresses the management, operational, and technical aspects of protecting federal information and information systems. We will categorize each system by three levels of risk: high, moderate, or low. The assigned level of risk indicates the baseline level of protection that needs to be identified, defined, and applied during the C&A phase I. Once the security categorizations along with the risk assessment (RA) of the GSSs and MAs are determined, the level of protection is identified in the system security plan (SSP).

System Security Plans (SSPs)

The technical team will provide system security plans (SSPs) by defining GSS and MA certification boundaries. In this case, the SSP for the GSSs and MAs will be used as a guideline, to the extent that data are relevant to the GSS and MA environments. For example, continuity planning for physical facilities might be similar if the systems are to be installed as a replacement for a client-server environment. Following the system definition, the SSP documents the agreements related to system security control and security measures arrived at by the

- System owner
- User representative
- Designated accreditation authority (DAA) or his or her designated representative
- Certification agent
- The technical team
- Other interested parties

For example, the SSP will identify the need for, the placement of, and the type of security controls to be provided to protect information system resources. Technical team views security controls as the key to management, operational, and technical safeguards and countermeasures identified for the information system. We will provide an SSP that maintains necessary security controls without creating undue user disruption or administrative burden. The SSP is the single document that acts as the authority for Information System Security (ISS)-related matters concerning each system and the applied protection schemes.

Since the SSP addresses the risks that the environment places upon the system, the SSP task will be addressed in conjunction with the associated system categorization and RA so that the risks identified are addressed and mitigated.

Risk Assessments (RAs)

In performing the risk assessments (RAs) for GSSs and MAs, the technical team will employ the organization approved RA methodology and make maximum use of the various tools identified in the rules of engagement (ROE) to discover the risk within the information system. The risk management process is a living process that continues throughout the life cycle of each GSS or MA and should be updated as a minimum on an annual cycle (Figure 13.4).

The application of those automated tools will generally follow NIST guidelines, in particular SP 800-30, *Risk Management Guide for Information Technology Systems.*

The organization RA methodology provides a baseline measurement of the target system's security controls. Therefore, this assessment provides management with the capability to make informed decisions for allocating IT program resources needed to fulfill the business requirements. In part, these decisions are reflected in the SSP as security appliances. The first step in the RA methodology is to characterize each system. Characterizing is the process used to define the business case for the system, which defines the system's

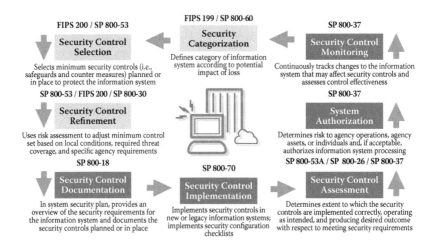

Figure 13.4 Risk management flow.

function and importance to the program and to the organization's overall mission. Key activities in managing enterprise-level risk—risk resulting from the operation of an information system—consist of

- *Categorizing* the information system
- *Selecting* a set of minimum (baseline) security controls
- *Refining* the security control set based on risk assessment
- *Documenting* security controls in system security plan
- *Implementing* the security controls in the information system
- *Assessing* the security controls
- *Determining* agency-level risk and risk acceptability
- *Authorizing* information system operation
- *Monitoring* security controls on a continuous basis

As part of the RA, the technical team's initial vulnerability assessment, as shown in Figure 13.5, is used to lessen the impacts of system security deficiencies discovered later in the C&A phase I approach. Early identification provides the opportunity to take corrective action prior to later assessment phases. The vulnerability assessments are conducted within the system's firewall boundary. This assessment is directed at discovering such items as improper OS configurations, missing OS or system patches, and missing or blank passwords.

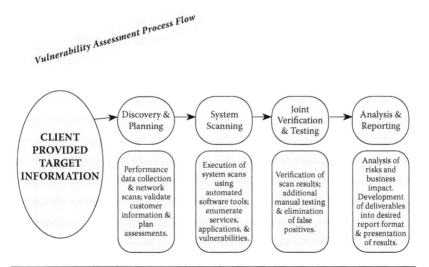

Figure 13.5 Vulnerability assessment flow diagram.

Penetration testing, another phase of the RA, is conducted from outside the organization's firewall, from a parent or subordinate organization, or from the Internet, and is directed at finding security holes in the organization's perimeter protections or at exploiting vulnerabilities that were previously identified. The tools typically employed by the technical team are NESSUS, SuperScan, AMAP, or other tools as approved by the client. Prior to conducting either of these tests, the technical team establishes the rules of engagement (ROE) for these tests, identifies and requests the organization's assistance from the system's security officer or administrator, and negotiates a memorandum of understanding (MOU) that contains the rules of engagement. Without this understanding, potential harm to the information system and false alarms might cause unexpected organizational concerns. The rules of engagement define what tests will be conducted, against what system, the duration, and the expected results. Since these tests can cause system harm in an uncontrolled environment, the technical team will control the test environment and keep test participants informed of test activities during the tests.

Both the vulnerability scans and penetration test are typically initiated from a technical team-provided laptop computer. The test tools identified previously are installed into a Linux operating environment on the laptop, and the laptop is connected to the customer network at one of two access points: (1) a network interface within the system firewall or (2) a network interface outside the system firewall. Although the vulnerability tests and penetration tests are independent, they will not be conducted simultaneously to reduce any adverse network risk.

Contingency Plans (CPs)

Contingency plans are an adjunct to the major investment or systems SSPs. Continuity of operation plans are a significant contributor to contingency planning. When practical, the technical team will attempt to validate each of the various contingency plans where such verification is nondisruptive to ongoing system operations. Contingency planning tests are generally performed under a separate contract due to the depth and length of the requirements.

Security Control Compliance Matrix (SCCM)

The security control compliance matrix (SCCM) will be developed by the technical team to document the associations between specific security requirements and specific security controls for each of the particular systems (Figure 13.6). Every security requirement identified in the particular information system's SSP is mapped to an appropriate security control within the baseline of security controls for that system. The security controls should include management, operational, and technical controls for the system, as it will be operated, as well as environmental controls and physical security controls. Once the security controls are identified, an SCCM shall be constructed. This matrix should list each security control, the reference from which

Control Number	Control Family Security Requirements	Control Requirements			
1	AC-1 Access Control Policy and Procedures				Corrective Action Plan
	Control: The organization develops, disseminates, and periodically reviews/updates: 1. A formal, documented, access control policy that addresses purpose, scope, roles, responsibilities, management commitment, and coordination among organizational entities, and compliance. 2. Formal, documented procedures to facilitate the implementation of the access control policy and associated access controls.	Compliant	Partially Implemented	Not Compliant	Not Applicable, Informational	
	AC-1.1 Examine organizational records or documents to determine if access control policy and procedures:					
	Exist	X				
	Are documented	X				
	Are disseminated to appropriate elements within the organization	X				

Figure 13.6   Sample security control compliance matrix.

the security control was derived, and whether or not the control has been implemented. The SCCM is developed during phase I and shall be implemented during phase II (security test and evaluation [ST&E]) and submitted as part of the certification package. Traceability requires unique identifiers for each requirement and system.

The technical team will extract individual security requirements that are identified in the SSP, define their application, identify possible mapping, and provide the applicable security appliance or control, security control.

Standard Operating Procedures (SOPs)

Standard operating procedures (SOPs) augment the SFUG, the TFM, or both by providing the step-by-step procedures to perform activities that are not spelled out in either of these documents. For example, the TFM may note the requirements for preventative maintenance on a backup or uninterruptible power supply (UPS). The TFM requirement is generally broadly specified to address all UPSs in the organization or major investment. However, a UPS applied to a desktop workstation is typically significantly different from a UPS applied to a network server. The workstation UPS SOPs will provide the details of the preventative maintenance to be performed, including a maintenance schedule. The SOP may also detail how corrective maintenance of the UPS is to be performed. SOPs may contain detailed checklists that must be followed or illustrate details of activities to be accomplished.

Privacy Impact Assessment (PIA)

Privacy impact assessments (PIAs) must be conducted on systems that process privacy act information or information in identifiable form (IIF). In the context of process, this term encompasses all elements of a modern information system and includes storing, handling, manipulating, and transferring an individual's personal (or privacy act-defined) information. The technical team, as part of its due diligence in understanding the function of the GSSs and MAs, will independently assess the privacy act data included across the GSSs and MAs, and the process by which they are managed. The technical team will work with the contracting officer technical representative (COTR) to modify the PIA requirements if there is a discrepancy between the requested PIA and the system processing privacy act data.

In some instances, an affirmative determination that a major investment system processes privacy act–controlled information may have a "feedback" affect upon the SSP, and further, the security controls that are required for that application. Should this be the case, the parties involved in negotiating the SSP (system owner, user representative, certification agent, DAA, etc.) will be notified of the discrepancy and the technical team recommendations for remedial action.

Configuration Management Plan (CMP)

The configuration management plan (CMP) will set forth the formal requirements for maintaining the system baseline configuration. The technical team will take into account the CM procedures used in managing the GSSs and MAs, and the current documentation requirements of the organization guidance. The baseline carries on the system description established for and contained in the SSP and follows guidelines established by the organization. It is anticipated that the CMP will be an evolution of the current process for management of the GSSs and MAs to address the configuration control requirements for the new system. The technical team will define and prepare a CMP that addresses the physical configuration of the system, both hardware and software as appropriate, including the certification boundaries and security controls for the system as well as supporting documentation for the baseline configuration. This supporting documentation includes the C&A documentation defined herein and elsewhere.

In addition, the CMP will identify and define the processes by which changes to the baseline configuration can be proposed, evaluated, approved/denied, and incorporated into the system. The technical team will provide an executive summary of changes recommended to the process used for the systems. This process will ensure that the approved system configuration can be identified by any of the key participants for the SSP at any time. This continuous baseline definition will support the determination for system recertification and reaccreditation.

Service Level Agreements (SLAs)

The service level agreement is an agreement between the service provider and the client. The agreement identifies the level of service that the hosting agency will provide and could be identified in packages (gold, silver, bronze), specific sequences of events, or other agreed upon events between the host and client. A service level agreement must be signed by designated representatives of both organizations. SLAs can be inter- or intraorganizational/department as required by the designated representatives.

General Process Phase II: Security Test and Evaluation (ST&E)

The security test and evaluation process (phase II) of the C&A process is the verification of phase I activity and security controls. Phase II consists of the following (Figure 13.7):

Documentation verification and correction
Security controls validation and recommendations
Development and recommendation of a plan of action and
    assistance in the milestone timelines (POA&M)
Provision of system architecture analysis
Software design analysis
Network analysis
Integrity analysis
Life cycle management analysis
Vulnerability assessment

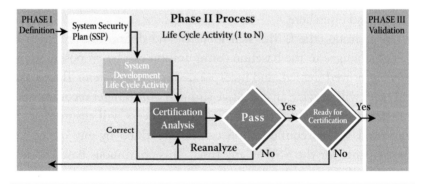

Figure 13.7   Phase II process.

Develop the Security Test and Evaluation (ST&E) Plan

In accordance with the organization C&A guide, and in consultation with the organization, a security test and evaluation plan shall be developed that

- Identifies those components of the major application (MA) or general support system (GSS) that are unique to the applications/systems in question and those that are either part of GSS or standard to the department, and therefore not requiring analysis during this review.
- Derives test objectives from security controls identified in phase I C&A activities related to the application-specific components or GSS. The test objectives should correspond to the appropriate requirements to test the security features of software unique to the application, as well as all administrative and procedural security requirements of the applications and associated interfaces.

Execute the ST&E Plan

After the ST&E plan has been approved by the COTR, the review procedures in the plan should be executed. An important part of the ST&E is the careful review of security-related documentation, such as the risk assessment (RA), system security plan (SSP), and Security Features User Guide (SFUG). These documents should be reviewed to ensure that they are

1. Developed in accordance with the appropriate organization and federal guidance
2. Up to date and usable for their intended purpose

During analysis, one person from the system owner's office should witness all ST&E activities to ensure that all procedures are properly executed.

Create the ST&E Report and Recommend Countermeasures

After the testing activities are complete, any findings from the review will be documented in an ST&E report. The report should identify which controls are complete, which security controls are only partially implemented, and those controls that are either not implemented or are ineffective. These results will be used as input to update the risk assessment.

After the ST&E report is complete, the system owner and the program manager should discuss the appropriate countermeasures to be implemented. These countermeasures should address any security requirements that were found to be not implemented or ineffective. Upon approval of the ST&E results the technical team will assist the client with the development of the plan of action and milestones (POA&M).

Update the Risk Assessment

The technical team will review the results from the ST&E to recommend updates to the risk assessment and determine the remaining risk for the system once corrective actions have taken place to address findings from the ST&E. Recommended updates to the risk assessment should be included in the form of an addendum to the original risk assessment report. Risk should be determined for both individual findings and the overall system or application. This risk determination will be included as part of the certification package. Both the organization Risk assessment methodology and NIST SP 800-30 will be used to ensure that all necessary risk assessment areas are completed.

Update the Security Plan

Using the guidance in NIST SP 800-18, the technical team will make recommendations for changes to the SSP to reflect the results of the ST&E activities and the final risk assessment. Any countermeasures implemented as a result of the ST&E findings should be added to the list of system security controls.

Document Certification Findings

Once the certification activities are complete, the technical team will work with the application owner's certification representative to document the findings from the certification process in a security evaluation report (SER). This report will summarize the findings and other relevant security issues identified during certification activities.

General Management and Methodologies

Employed Methodologies

The technical team methodology for development, review, and enhancement of the required C&A documents blends several methodologies used successfully in numerous engagements. An information gathering phase is performed based on the system management methodology. This key initial step ensures that the scope and boundaries of the systems targeted for the C&A process are fully understood, that all existing vendor and organization documentation about the systems is obtained and available, and that undocumented, institutional knowledge is gathered through structured interviews with management and system administrators/users. The technical team's structured data gathering/interview process is a significant factor for successful C&A of a system. Our methodology ensures that complete knowledge of the GSS and MA major investment operating environments are obtained and recorded efficiently to support the document preparation phase of the effort, as follows:

1. *Select appropriate methods and tools to develop the documentation.* After the information-gathering phase, the technical team will identify opportunities for use of automation or other tools to simplify the data recording and document generation process. For example, commonly used data (e.g., location address) may be entered once into a repository and linked to multiple documents that require the same data content. This methodology reduces the amount of data entry required to generate the documents, improves the quality of the documents by limiting the opportunity for typographical errors, and simplifies the initial quality assurance and ongoing maintenance of the completed documents.

2. *Have senior technical writers actively participate in planning, developing, and maintaining documentation.* The technical team staffing plan includes experienced technical writers that are dedicated to this effort throughout the entire project. They will actively participate in the information gathering, work planning, and documentation preparation and review tasks. In particular, the senior technical writer will track review

comments, technical changes, and other enhancements to ensure that lessons learned from review of documentation of one system are incorporated, if appropriate, into the remaining documentation.

3. *Ensure that preliminary versions of the documentation are reviewed by the customer early in the process.* Because of the number of different documents required for this effort, the technical team's program manager (PM) will provide preliminary versions of selected/typical documents for review by the customer. All feedback received will be incorporated into both documents that were reviewed and the remaining documents being prepared. This step will improve the overall quality of the final set of documentation while minimizing the number of unique documentation reviews that the organization staff must perform.

4. *Final versions of the documentation are verified against the system to which they apply.* Before GSS and MA draft final documents are submitted for management review, the technical team will verify that the documentation accurately reflects the way the system is installed and performs. This verification will include a combination of desk checking and hands-on verification. Any required updates or enhancements will be incorporated into all of the appropriate documents.

5. *The documentation undergoes peer review.* Once the documentation has been verified against the system, a team of technical writers will perform an independent review of the draft to ensure that the format and flow of information are consistent and user-friendly to the target audience.

6. *The documentation is managed and controlled.* All documentation will be maintained by the senior technical writer under strict version control to ensure that only approved changes, in accordance with the review process, are incorporated. This process will also provide a continuous improvement mechanism to apply lessons learned from the testing and review of one document into the remaining documentation sets.

7. *The final documentation is reviewed and approved by the customer, end users, and certification agent, as appropriate.* In accordance with the Statement of Work (SOW), draft documentation that has passed the technical team quality reviews, including

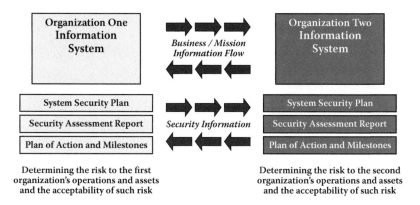

Figure 13.8 End-state security model.

peer reviews, will be submitted to the client management for review and comment. Comments are to be received within five business days of delivery of the draft. All comments received will be incorporated into the final version of the document.

Internal Review Procedures

As a part of our commitment to quality, the technical team has implemented procedures that encompass every aspect of the technical team management, from on-site quality task management reviews by the technical team PMs to peer review of deliverable documents. Our document preparation methodology calls for multiple rounds of customer, peer, and management review of deliverables, as well as a hands-on verification of the usability of the document.

End-State Security Model

Figure 13.8 shows the end-state security model for security visibility among business/mission partners and the end-state objective. Once the end-state model has been obtained, each organization can negotiate the interconnection agreement and determine the level of trust between the organizations.

The objective is to achieve *visibility* into prospective business/mission partner's information security programs before critical/sensitive communications begin—establishing levels of security due diligence.

Appendix A: References (NIST)

NIST SP 800-100: *Information Security Handbook: A Guide for Managers*

NIST SP 800-87: *Codes for the Identification of Federal and Federally-Assisted Organizations*

NIST SP 800-86 (Draft): *Guide to Computer and Network Data Analysis: Applying Forensic Techniques to Incident Response*

NIST SP 800-85: *PIV Middleware and PIV Card Application Conformance Test Guidelines*

NIST SP 800-84 (Draft): *Guide to Single-Organization IT Exercises*

NIST SP 800-83 (Draft): *Guide to Malware Incident Prevention and Handling*

NIST SP 800-81 (Draft): *Secure Domain Name System (DNS) Deployment Guide*

NIST SP 800-79: *Guidelines for the Certification and Accreditation of PIV Card Issuing Organizations*

NIST SP 800-78: *Cryptographic Algorithms and Key Sizes for Personal Identity Verification*

NIST SP 800-77 (Draft): *Guide to IPsec VPNs*

NIST SP 800-76 (Draft): *Biometric Data Specification for Personal Identity Verification*

NIST SP 800-73: *Interfaces for Personal Identity Verification*

NIST SP 800-72: *Guidelines on PDA Forensics*

NIST SP 800-70: *The NIST Security Configuration Checklists Program*

NIST SP 800-68 (Draft): *Guidance for Securing Microsoft Windows XP Systems for IT Professionals: A NIST Security Configuration Checklist*

NIST SP 800-67: *Recommendation for the Triple Data Encryption Algorithm (TDEA) Block Cipher*

NIST SP 800-66: *An Introductory Resource Guide for Implementing the Health Insurance Portability and Accountability Act (HIPAA) Security Rule*

NIST SP 800-65: *Integrating Security into the Capital Planning and Investment Control Process*

NIST SP 800-64: *Security Considerations in the Information System Development Life Cycle*

NIST SP 800-63: *Electronic Authentication Guideline: Recommendations of the National Institute of Standards and Technology*

NIST SP 800-61: *Computer Security Incident Handling Guide*

NIST SP 800-60: *Guide for Mapping Types of Information and Information Systems to Security Categories*

NIST SP 800-59: *Guideline for Identifying an Information System as a National Security System*

NIST SP 800-58: *Security Considerations for Voice Over IP Systems*

NIST SP 800-57: *Recommendation on Key Management*

NIST SP 800-56 (Draft): *Recommendation on Key Establishment Schemes*

NIST SP 800-55: *Security Metrics Guide for Information Technology Systems*

NIST SP 800-53: *Recommended Security Controls for Federal Information Systems*
Annex 1: Consolidated Security Controls–Low Baseline
Annex 2: Consolidated Security Controls—Moderate Baseline
Annex 3: Consolidated Security Controls–High Baseline

NIST SP 800-52: *Guidelines for the Selection and Use of Transport Layer Security (TLS) Implementations*

NIST SP 800-51: *Use of the Common Vulnerabilities and Exposures (CVE) Vulnerability Naming Scheme*

NIST SP 800-50: *Building an Information Technology Security Awareness and Training Program*

NIST SP 800-49: *Federal S/MIME V3 Client Profile*

NIST SP 800-48: *Wireless Network Security: 802.11, Bluetooth, and Handheld Devices*

NIST SP 800-47: *Security Guide for Interconnecting Information Technology Systems*

NIST SP 800-46: *Security for Telecommuting and Broadband Communications*

NIST SP 800-45: *Guidelines on Electronic Mail Security*

NIST SP 800-44: *Guidelines on Securing Public Web Servers*

NIST SP 800-42: *Guideline on Network Security Testing*

NIST SP 800-41: *Guidelines on Firewalls and Firewall Policy*

NIST SP 800-40 (Draft): *Version 2—Creating a Patch and Vulnerability Management Program*

NIST SP 800-40: *Procedures for Handling Security Patches*

NIST SP 800-38C: *Recommendation for Block Cipher Modes of Operation: The CCM Mode for Authentication and Confidentiality*

NIST SP 800-38B: *Recommendation for Block Cipher Modes of Operation: The CMAC Mode for Authentication*

NIST SP 800-38A: *Recommendation for Block Cipher Modes of Operation—Methods and Techniques*

NIST SP 800-37: *Guide for the Security Certification and Accreditation of Federal Information Systems*

NIST SP 800-36: *Guide to Selecting Information Security Products*

NIST SP 800-35: *Guide to Information Technology Security Services*

NIST SP 800-34: *Contingency Planning Guide for Information Technology Systems*

NIST SP 800-33: *Underlying Technical Models for Information Technology Security*

NIST SP 800-32: *Introduction to Public Key Technology and the Federal PKI Infrastructure*

NIST SP 800-31: *Intrusion Detection Systems (IDS)*

NIST SP 800-30: *Risk Management Guide for Information Technology Systems*

NIST SP 800-29: *A Comparison of the Security Requirements for Cryptographic Modules in FIPS 140-1 and FIPS 140-2*

NIST SP 800-28: *Guidelines on Active Content and Mobile Code*

NIST SP 800-27: *Engineering Principles for Information Technology Security (A Baseline for Achieving Security), Revision A*

NIST SP 800-26: *Guide for Information Security Program Assessments and System Reporting Form*

NIST SP 800-26: *Security Self-Assessment Guide for Information Technology Systems*
Revised NIST SP 800-26: *System Questionnaire with NIST SP 800-53 References and Associated Security Control Mappings*

NIST SP 800-25: *Federal Agency Use of Public Key Technology for Digital Signatures and Authentication*

NIST SP 800-24: *PBX Vulnerability Analysis: Finding Holes in Your PBX before Someone Else Does*

NIST SP 800-23: *Guideline to Federal Organizations on Security Assurance and Acquisition/Use of Tested/Evaluated Products*

NIST SP 800-21: *Guideline for Implementing Cryptography in the Federal Government*

NIST SP 800-18 (Draft): *Revision 1, Guide for Developing Security Plans for Federal Information Systems*

NIST SP 800-18: *Guide for Developing Security Plans for Information Technology Systems*

NIST SP 800-16: *Information Technology Security Training Requirements: A Role- and Performance-Based Model*

NIST SP 800-15: *Minimum Interoperability Specification for PKI Components (MISPC), Version 1*

NIST SP 800-14: *Generally Accepted Principles and Practices for Securing Information Technology Systems*

NIST SP 800-13: *Telecommunications Security Guidelines for Telecommunications Management Network*

NIST SP 800-12: *An Introduction to Computer Security: The NIST Handbook*

Appendix B: References (FIPS)

With the passage of the Federal Information Security Management Act (FISMA) of 2002, there is no longer a statutory provision to allow for agencies to waive mandatory Federal Information Processing Standards (FIPS). The waiver provision had been included in the Computer Security Act of 1987; however, FISMA supersedes that act. Therefore, the references to the waiver process contained in many of the FIPS listed below are no longer operative.

Note: Not all FIPS are mandatory; consult the applicability section of each FIPS for details. FIPS do not apply to national security systems (as defined in FISMA).

FIPS 140-1: *Security Requirements for Cryptographic Modules*
FIPS 140-2: *Security Requirements for Cryptographic Modules*
    Annex A: Approved Security Functions
    Annex B: Approved Protection Profiles
    Annex C: Approved Random Number Generators
    Annex D: Approved Key Establishment Techniques
FIPS 181: *Automated Password Generator*
FIPS 186-2: *Digital Signature Standard (DSS)*
FIPS 188: *Standard Security Labels for Information Transfer*
FIPS 190: *Guideline for the Use of Advanced Authentication Technology Alternatives*

FIPS 191: *Guideline for the Analysis of Local Area Network Security*

FIPS 196: *Entity Authentication Using Public Key Cryptography*

FIPS 197: *Advanced Encryption Standard*

FIPS 199: *Standards for Security Categorization of Federal Information and Information Systems*

FIPS 200: *Minimum Security Requirements for Federal Information and Information Systems* (replaces NIST SP 800-53)

FIPS 201: *Personal Identity Verification for Federal Employees and Contractors*

Appendix C: Sample Certification Statement

Introduction

Brief description of system and interconnections.

Statement of Compliance

The *agency system* complies with the requirements of FIPS 199, 200, and NIST SP 800-53 and the requirements of OMB Circular A-130. The data contained within the *agency system* are a low-rated major application that consists of a tiered architecture web interface to an SQL 2000 SP4 database. The *agency system* is a stand-alone system that has interconnection agreements and memorandums of agreement in place with the 12 banks and 1 federal system. The interconnections are protected by a VPN, IP filtering, and active directory authentication. Users of the system are not authorized to write to the system directly.

Control Family	Control	Partially Implemented	Not Compliant
M	CA-3, Information Systems Connections	√	
M	PL-5, Privacy Impact Assessment		√

(Continued)

Control Family	Control	Partially Implemented	Not Compliant
0	PS-2, Position Categorization		√
T	AU-9, Protection of Audit Information		√

Certification Statement

I certify that the *agency system* meets all federal security requirements as it operates in its current environment. A review of the security controls will be conducted upon any major operating environment changes.

_____   _____

Certifying Company   Date

Appendix D: Sample Rules of Engagement

The rules of engagement for this vulnerability assessment are designed to document the procedures and framework for agency system scanning conducted during the security test and evaluation (ST&E) scheduled for date of evaluation. Computer Security Consulting, Inc. (CSCI) and the agency system security manager will jointly collaborate while performing this vulnerability assessment. The rules of engagement establish the scope by defining targets, time frame, rules, and points of contact. They also provide authorization to proceed. For questions concerning the content of this document, please contact company rep at email.com.

Scope of Objective

Our scanning procedures are designed to focus on the agency system and servers designated and approved for scanning by the agency system security officer. Our objective is to identify and inventory any exposures or weaknesses found in the specified targets as a subset activity within the overall agency system ST&E task.

Our test procedures employ nondestructive, minimally invasive techniques limited to IP reconnaissance, vulnerability mapping, and resource enumeration. No files or data will be modified or changed. Furthermore, this assessment is not likely to disable users or deny service. For the purposes of this penetration procedure, successful penetration is defined by demonstrating any one of the following:

- Remotely or locally obtain the ability to copy, modify, or delete system configuration files.

(*Note:* Under no circumstances will any data or files be modified or deleted.)

- Remotely or locally view, modify, or obtain password files.
- Obtain the ability to redirect traffic.

(*Note:* Under no circumstances will traffic be redirected.)

Evidence to support any weaknesses discovered will consist primarily of screen prints, session logs, or automated tool reports. We will evaluate vulnerabilities discovered during the scan and discuss with agency system the potential for further penetration testing.

Use of Automated Tools

We will direct the use of the automated probing and scanning tools, Nessus, WebSense, and Nmap, to determine system configurations, default settings, security settings, network services, and open ports on the agency resources. The tools will detect vulnerabilities on the scanned resources, including those vulnerabilities published by the Common Vulnerabilities and Exposures Database and the FBI/SANS Top 20 List.

Vulnerabilities tested by agency's scanning tools include, but are not limited to

- SMTP weaknesses
- IP fragmentation checks
- ICMP checks
- Odd protocol checks
- Port checks
- NETBIOS vulnerabilities
- WC service vulnerabilities

- HTTP vulnerabilities
- NIS weaknesses
- Protocol spoofing checks

We will carefully analyze the results of the scans in order to verify the detection of vulnerabilities and ensure accurate reporting. False positives are extremely difficult to determine, and system administrators should assist in identifying possible applications that might utilize unknown findings.

Terms of Testing

The following are agreed upon terms that will be in place as part of the penetration test:

- All network scanning and penetration procedures will be accomplished within the specified time period as outlined in the section "Time Line."
- Penetration testing will be conducted during normal business hours, defined as 8:00 a.m. through 5:00 p.m.
- The IP addresses are identified in the kickoff meeting or meeting with the agency security manager as identified for the penetration testing; only those addresses listed will be tested.
- The scans will simply determine what vulnerabilities may exist within the agency systems. We will not attempt to exploit these vulnerabilities or gain unauthorized access.
- A full network scan will not be performed. A targeted system scan will be completed and limited to the addresses on the server lists that contain target machines, so as to control and further minimize load on the network infrastructure.
- When high-risk vulnerabilities are discovered, they will be exploited only to determine their validity. No exploits will be attempted beyond gaining access to the operating system or application.
- Absent of log file overflows, we will refrain from denial-of-service attempts unless specifically authorized by agency personnel involved.
- The agency security officer may, at any point in time, exercise the option to cancel scanning activities.

During our attempts to penetrate the agency infrastructure, we will observe the following rules of behavior to minimize the impact on agency systems resources:

- No untested software tools or techniques will be employed.
- All files and directories can be scanned for file names and attributes.
- System-level and software files can be viewed to demonstrate vulnerabilities, but not altered, deleted, or executed.
- No updates or modifications will be made to system or data files.
- User files and any other data contained in agency's information systems that are part of an agency system of records on individuals to which CSCI obtains access will be kept confidential in a manner consistent with the privacy act (5 U.S.C. 5552a) and the applicable agency regulation (45 C.F.R. Part 613).
- Utmost care will be exercised not to disable user IDs. For any user ID found to be inadvertently disabled, we will notify the appropriate agency representative to ensure the prompt restoration of access.
- Any procedure that may have potential negative impact on network traffic or interruption will be avoided.
- All information about this penetration test, such as the information system's vulnerabilities and potential security compromises, will be kept completely confidential and released only to agency's points of contacts.

Notification Procedures

Prior to scanning, we will provide agency with all IP addresses from hosts to be used for the scanning (see "IP Ranges" on the next page). The IP range list was approved by the security officer, agency. Agency's staff should block any activity detected outside the scope of this test unless your staff believes we are performing it. If so, contact us to determine if the detected activity is related to the penetration test. If you are unable to contact us, we suggest blocking the IP addresses as a means to safeguard agency's system resources.

Reporting

We will incorporate the results of our penetration study into our security test and evaluation report. We will also provide you and system owners with a briefing, summarizing the results of the study, detailed scan reports, and recommended corrective actions.

Critical vulnerabilities: At the end of the scan the scan data will be parsed for critical and severe vulnerabilities. These are vulnerabilities that require immediate attention. These vulnerabilities will be passed to the security office in the RAW text format output of the scan tool.

Other vulnerabilities: These will be reviewed, over the course of the next 48 hours, and any areas of concern will be identified. If there appears to be further areas of major concern (rated high on 10 or more instances on the same server), a memo will be drafted stating the concern and the server(s) in question.

- **Draft report:** Draft report will be delivered to agency security manager within five days of scan.
- **Final report:** The final scan report will be delivered three business days following written/markup comments on the draft.

IP Ranges

Our scans will be limited to the following:

Target System	IP Address	System Name	Operating System	Database Scan
				☐ Yes ☐ No
				☐ Yes ☐ No
				☐ Yes ☐ No
				☐ Yes ☐ No

I have agreed to the above rules and penetration test objects.

_____

Signature (Approving Official)　　　　　　　Title　　　　　　Date

Index

T - #0781 - 101024 - C0 - 234/156/12 [14] - CB - 9781439841594 - Gloss Lamination